EARLY ISRAEL IN
RECENT HISTORY WRITING

STUDIES IN BIBLICAL THEOLOGY

EARLY ISRAEL
IN RECENT
HISTORY WRITING

A Study in Method

JOHN BRIGHT

McCormick Professor of Hebrew
and Old Testament Interpretation
Union Theological Seminary
Richmond Virginia

SCM PRESS LTD
56 BLOOMSBURY STREET
LONDON

First published 1956

Printed in Great Britain
by W. & J. Mackay & Co. Ltd., Chatham

To

the Members

of the Biblical Colloquium

before whom certain portions of this
study were read at their meeting in
Pittsburgh, Pa., in November of 1954.
I wish to thank them for their friendly
interest, which emboldened me to
continue my labours on the subject,
and also for their numerous criticisms
and suggestions

CONTENTS

I INTRODUCTION
  The Nature of the Problem   11

II THE SCHOOL OF ALT AND NOTH
  A Summary   34

III YEHEZKEL KAUFMANN
  A Summary and Evaluation   56

IV THE SCHOOL OF ALT AND NOTH
  A Critical Evaluation   79

V CONCLUSIONS   111

  INDEX OF BIBLICAL REFERENCES   127

ABBREVIATIONS

BA	*The Biblical Archaeologist*
BAC	Y. Kaufmann, *The Biblical Account of the Conquest of Palestine* (Jerusalem, The Magnes Press, 1953)
BASOR	*Bulletin of the American Schools of Oriental Research*
BJRL	*Bulletin of the John Rylands Library*
BZAW	Beihefte zur *Zeitschrift für die alttestamentliche Wissenschaft*
GI	M. Noth, *Geschichte Israels* (Göttingen, Vandenhoeck & Ruprecht, 1950)
GVI	R. Kittel, *Geschichte des Volkes Israel* (Stuttgart, W. Kohlhammer, 3 Vols.; Vol. I, 7th ed., 1932)
HTR	*Harvard Theological Review*
JAOS	*Journal of the American Oriental Society*
JBL	*Journal of Biblical Literature*
JNES	*Journal of Near Eastern Studies*
KS	A. Alt, *Kleine Schriften zur Geschichte des Volkes Israel* (München, C. H. Beck'sche Verlagsbuchhandlung, 2 Vols. 1953)
PJB	*Palästinajahrbuch*
UG	M. Noth, *Überlieferungsgeschichte des Pentateuchs* (Stuttgart, W. Kohlhammer, 1948)
ZAW	*Zeitschrift für die alttestamentliche Wissenschaft*
ZDPV	*Zeitschrift des deutschen Palästina-vereins*

CHAPTER ONE

INTRODUCTION

The Nature of the Problem

I

THE present study has to do with a problem of method that decisively affects both the writing and the understanding of the history of Israel. It is a problem that arises in connexion with the earliest history of Israel and the early traditions of Israel—the traditions of patriarchs, exodus and conquest—as these are found in the Hexateuch. It might be stated succinctly in the form of a question: by what method may one evaluate the historical worth of these traditions, and in what manner, and to what degree, may one use them, together with other evidence, in reconstructing the origins and early history of the Hebrew people? While it should hardly be necessary to warn the reader not to expect to find any final answer to that question in these pages—to pretend to know a final answer would scarcely be less than arrogant—it is hoped that what will be said will serve to make the nature of the problem clear. It is hoped, too, that certain conclusions regarding its solution, both of a negative and a positive nature, may emerge.

Now beyond question, of all the problems that beset the writing of the history of Israel, the one just raised is easily the most crucial, the most sweeping, and the most difficult of solution. Nor is it without profound theological significance. It is because the casual reader might be tempted at first glance to think it a purely academic matter of no practical concern to theologian or pastor, that it is necessary to stress this. Old Testament theology is primarily a theology of events; it is concerned with events and the interpretation of those events in the light of faith. And of all these events, none are more fundamental to the theology of the Old Testament than those described in the Hexateuch. Here it is told how God summoned a people to himself and led them out of dire bondage, that they might live in covenant with him under his law, and that he might give to them the land already promised to their fathers. All Old Testament believing takes its start from this point. And, although one may say that the theological interpretation is of greater significance than the events themselves, the actual history can never be a matter of indifference to the theologian. For Old Testament theology rests in history quite as much as does that of the New. Of neither history can the theologian say: it does not matter.

One's reconstruction of early Israel's history and faith does, in fact, matter greatly. Not only is a satisfying picture of the history and religion of that particular period dependent on it; one's total interpretation of all of Israel's subsequent history, political, institutional and spiritual, is certain to be deeply coloured by it. Indeed, the degree of historic continuity that one is prepared to find in Israel's religion and, therewith, the degree of unity that one may allow to Old Testament theology, is involved. In short, it is a problem that vitally affects one's understanding of the Old Testament both as a whole and in all of its parts.

Yet, for all that, it is impossible to resist the conclusion that it is a problem that has never satisfactorily been solved. Certainly no solution has been advanced that has received anything like universal acceptance. There is no semblance of unanimity on the point to be found in the books on the subject available today. Indeed, he who is even moderately acquainted with this literature, and who takes into account the differences in aim and scope of the various works in question, is likely to be struck by two things: on the one hand, a remarkable general agreement in the handling of Israel's history from, say, the rise of the monarchy onward; and, on the other, an equally remarkable lack of agreement where the early period is concerned.

This is not to say, of course, that the later portions of Israel's history evoke no disagreement, or that all treatments here become mere dittos of one another, so that to read one is to read all. Far from it! On the contrary, from end to end of Israel's history there are a thousand places where there is room for difference of opinion in interpreting the evidence, with consequent divergences in the telling of the story. This is, and must always be, the case. It is certain that none of us will ever live to see it otherwise. What is more, the later periods no less than the earlier allow play for the most sweeping differences in the all-over understanding of Israel's faith and in the evaluation of the traditions. For example, the handling of the prophet movement as a whole and in detail will be conditioned inevitably by the way in which the religion of early

Israel has been interpreted. Or, again, a scepticism regarding early tradition is likely to be matched by a scepticism regarding later tradition (notably the Chronicler!) That is to say, some scholars are far more inclined than others to credit the Bible tradition, in absence of evidence to the contrary, and this is reflected throughout their work.

Yet all this but serves to point up the fact that it is precisely the early period that is the rub. It is there that histories of Israel go farthest apart from one another. In the handling of the later period, disagreements tend to be disagreements in detail. The farther one reads from the beginning in the various treatments, the narrower the *areas* of disagreement tend to become. Once the historian has gotten Israel finally settled in Palestine and organized into the classical Twelve-Clan League, one senses that he has begun to tread on firm and familiar ground. True, problems confront him at every step, but they are problems such as he feels competent to deal with: they are problems not essentially different from those that beset the writing of the history of any people. He marches, in other words, ever more into the full light of history. Israel is now a people settled on her land, her presence attested by tangible archaeological evidence, and witnessed to by contemporary records both in her own scriptures and in the inscriptions of her neighbours that grow increasingly profuse as time goes on.

But when one faces about and looks back to the events of conquest, exodus and before, all is different. It is not merely that the problem before the historian is more difficult in degree; it is totally different in kind. For here one has passed from the history of Israel back into her pre-history. It is the period when, as far as Israel is concerned, no contemporary records exist, for little or nothing in the Old Testament scriptures can be proved *in its present form* to be so old.[1] Records of the neighbouring nations do not mention her.[2] Since she was not as yet settled on her land, Palestinian archaeology affords no direct witness to her. As for the archaeology of the ancient Near East in general, while it has most brilliantly illuminated the age of Israel's origins, and provided

---

[1] I stress the words 'in its present form'. That many of the traditions, poems and laws of the Hexateuch had their origin in the period of the conquest and before, few today would question. But we read them in documents of the tenth century and later.

[2] As is well known, the earliest mention of Israel in a contemporary inscription is found in the Marniptah Stele of the late thirteenth century.

evidence in profusion for the understanding of those origins, it does not fix the details of Israel's pre-history save in a most general way. The result is that when the historian turns back to tell of how Israel came to her land, of the nature of the religion she presumably brought with her and how she got it, of the fortunes of her ancestors in a period yet more remote, we sense his unhappiness. He is moving in a realm of conjecture and theory and he is not at home in it. He feels himself faced with a dilemma: to leave the whole matter aside with as few words as possible, or to present a more or less elaborate hypothetical reconstruction of the course of events. These last have been offered in great numbers but, needless to say, no two of them agree save perhaps in broad outline. The best of them are quite reasonable, the worst quite wild; all are incapable of proof in detail.

This is not to say, of course, that Israel possessed no recollection of this period. To the contrary! She preserved a tradition of her origins, with a profusion and precision of detail, to which the ancient world offers no parallel whatever. There is nothing in any ancient literature to compare with the stories of the patriarchs, the exodus, the wilderness wandering and the conquest as told in the first six books of the Bible. Here we are given the history of Israel's beginnings as that history was preserved in Hebrew tradition, and believed by the Hebrews themselves. But these are certainly not contemporary historical records. Not only did they not reach their present form until centuries after the events described,[1] they are not cast in the form of historical annals and cannot be evaluated as such. They form the Epic of the Hebrew people; they preserve the national traditions of that people.[2]

But how are these traditions to be evaluated? What historical recollections, if any, do they contain? It has been a question without agreed answer. At one extreme, there have been those who have accepted them as fully—or substantially—historical, and have with confidence reconstructed the story of early Israel (and even the biographies of the ancestors) on the basis of them, much as the Bible tells it. At the other extreme, some have allowed them little or no historical value at all. The majority of historians, how-

---

[1] That is, of course, unless one subscribes to full Mosaic authorship—and even then the patriarchal narratives lie some centuries before the writing.

[2] I shall resolutely adhere to the neutral term 'tradition' in referring to these stories. It means simply 'what is handed down', and does not prejudice the question of historical worth. Cf. F. James, *Personalities of the Old Testament* (New York, Chas. Scribner's Sons, 1939), 4.

ever, fall somewhere in between: the traditions are not historical records, but they have to some degree a basis in history and preserve some historical reminiscences. But to what degree is this so, and how is that to be ascertained? Here, again, one finds no agreed answer. Evaluation of tradition, and consequent reconstruction of the events, differs with each scholar consulted. As a result, treatments of the patriarchs, for example, vary from a rather full reliance upon the traditions, all the way to an extreme scepticism that denies the patriarchs historical existence and reduces them to mere clan eponyms—or even totem animals, mythical figures, or gods.[1] Though Moses is seldom these days relegated to the realm of the unhistorical, treatments of his work again vary from almost total nihilism to a rather complete acceptance of the exodus traditions. As for the religion of early Israel, it was on the one hand, the worship of a tribal god, a war god, a storm god, a volcano god—or what not; on the other hand, it was a full monotheism. In short, where the earliest history of Israel is concerned, one may find head-on clashes of opinion at almost every point, together with totally divergent reconstructions of the whole. Let the reader select the one that most pleases him or, with good precedent, make his own!

Now it must be stressed that this confusion reflects an unsolved problem of method. All these reconstructions, diverse as they are, are made on the basis of the same traditions and, taking into consideration the date of the work in question and the scholarly competence of its author, the same external evidence. The question is not, therefore, primarily one of the field of evidence, but of the evaluation of that evidence. In this last there is no observable consistency. One might almost gain the impression that each scholar selects from the traditions that which his best judgement and his predilections allow him to regard as historical—often little enough —and discards the rest. It is without doubt the most pressing problem confronting the historiography of Israel that the question of method as it applies to this problem be given an answer. By what objective controls are the early traditions of Israel to be evaluated? How can it be decided to what degree, and in what way, one may use them for the reconstruction of early Israelite history? What weight ought to be laid on archaeological evidence,

[1] I do not feel it necessary to document this and the following statements in detail. It is common knowledge that all these and others can be found in books produced in the last twenty-five years. I have no desire to take issue with any particular treatment at this point.

and how is this to be interpreted? Until these questions, and others like them, are answered to general satisfaction, it may safely be predicted that no history of Israel—or theology of the Old Testament—will ever be written which will be acceptable beyond the school of the author who produced it.

It is to this problem that the present study directs itself. As has been said, it pretends to offer no final solution, or even a consistent programme for gaining one. Still less will any fresh reconstruction of the early history of Israel be attempted here. What is offered is something far more modest, yet something which, it is hoped, may serve as a contribution to the problem of method. We shall first attempt to make clear the nature of the problem by a brief review of the ways in which it has been handled in the literature of the past quarter-century. The bulk of the study will then be given over to a critical evaluation of certain weighty attempts at its solution which have appeared within the last few years. It is possible that what will be said may seem to be in good part negative: a critical evaluation is to a degree necessarily so. But it is hoped that certain positive conclusions, and certain methodological principles may nevertheless emerge.

2

Any attempt to assay the manner in which the early history of Israel has been handled in the literature of recent years will run head on into the sheer mass of material available. Manifestly, it is impossible to list here every treatment that bears on the early traditions of Israel, or on some particular phase or problem of the early history. We shall confine ourselves to such attacks on the problem as have issued in systematic attempts to write the history of Israel, and which thus explicitly develop, or implicitly reflect, the method by which the early traditions are evaluated. Since some arbitrary limit must be set, we shall further confine ourselves to works issued within the past twenty-five years (from 1930 and onward). Even so, one is still embarrassed by the mass of material. Our listing cannot pretend to be complete, especially where popular manuals are concerned. The pen of the historian has not been dry in this quarter-century but has, on the contrary, poured forth books in the greatest profusion, varying in scope from the slim and popular to the fat and technical, and from all possible theological and critical viewpoints.

Nevertheless, while it would possibly be to speak subjectively, it would certainly be to echo a widespread feeling, if one were to say that no up-to-date and entirely satisfactory treatment of the subject exists today. I am aware that that statement may have an arrogant sound about it, and for that reason I stress its subjective nature. Others may quite possibly disagree. Yet the dissatisfaction is, I know, by no means peculiarly my own.

The 'standard' histories of Israel are now without exception badly out-of-date, so rapid has been the increase of knowledge. An up-to-date replacement for these works is a prime desideratum, but it needs the hand of a master scholar to write it.[1] *Facile princeps* among existing ones is, in my opinion, that of R. Kittel.[2] This is a work of first quality, marked by wide learning, sober critical judgement, and a command of the archaeological evidence available at the time of its writing. It stands head and shoulders above comparable works, and is still usable. But it is some thirty years out-of-date and, since the author is long dead, it is doubtful if it will again be revised. Of works in English of comparable bulk, we have those of Oesterley and Robinson, Lods, and Olmstead.[3] Each of these has its merits and demerits and, while the treatment of the early period in the three is by no means identical, there is a basic similarity: identical questions are raised. Furthermore, all are out-of-date and, the authors (save T. H. Robinson) being dead, revision is unlikely. In our period, too, there falls the latest revision of the classic work of Ed. Meyer.[4] This work is of such scope and brilliance that it requires no comment. But it is likewise out-of-date and the treatment of early Israel, which falls in the general pattern of the three works previously mentioned, needs radical revision.

The gap has been in a measure filled, from a Roman Catholic

[1] W. F. Albright, *From the Stone Age to Christianity* (London, Oxford University Press, 2nd ed. 1946) might be called the prolegomena to such a work. That Prof. Albright would go on to produce it is 'a consummation devoutly to be wished'.

[2] R. Kittel, *GVI* (see list of abbreviations). Since the 7th edition of Vol. I (1932) is merely a reprint of the 6th edition of 1923, this work properly falls outside our period. But it ought not to be omitted.

[3] Oesterley and Robinson, *A History of Israel* (Oxford, Clarendon Press, 2 Vols. 1932); A. Lods, *Israel: from the Beginnings to the Middle of the Eighth Century*, trans. by S. H. Hooke (London, Routledge, 1932); A. T. Olmstead, *History of Palestine and Syria* (New York, Chas. Scribner's Sons, 1931). The last work does not confine itself to Israel, but it should be listed here.

[4] Ed. Meyer, *Geschichte des Altertums*. The treatment of the relevant period of Israel's history falls in Vol. II: 2, 187–361 (Stuttgart and Berlin, J. G. Cotta'sche Buchhandlung, 2nd ed. 1931).

viewpoint, by the recent work of Ricciotti,[1] a work that may go far toward replacing the worthy, but now antiquated, work of Desnoyers.[2] Ricciotti's is a treatment of considerable learning and merit, but it is marred by a high chronology which, in a measure, renders it out-of-date even though new.[3] Its approach to the early history of Israel, while diametrically opposite to the preceding works, raises questions for different reasons. Finally, we have the monumental work of Y. Kaufmann,[4] primarily a history of Israel's religion, but a political history as well. Kaufmann's approach will be given extended discussion below.

To these large works must be added a number of smaller handbooks designed for the use of the theological student. Of these one stands out: that of Noth.[5] Noth's work is of such fundamental importance, and of such relentless method, that the greater part of this study will be devoted to it. Other manuals, Catholic, Protestant and Jewish, designed for classroom use and for the general public are too numerous to list.[6] Some of these are quite good indeed and, but for their brevity, might adequately fill the instructional gap.[7] Others, however, exhibit such a woeful lack of

---

[1] G. Ricciotti, *Histoire d'Israël*, French trans. by P. Auvray (Paris, A. & J. Picard et Cie., 2 Vols. new ed. 1947–48). A German edition has been issued, and now—so I am told—an English one.

[2] L. Desnoyers, *Histoire du peuple hébreu: des juges a la captivité* (Paris, Desclée de Brouwer et Cie. 3 Vols. 1922–30).

[3] This statement needs qualification. Formerly Ricciotti had placed Hammurabi in the twentieth century. In a sentence on page 14 of Vol. I of the new edition, he lowers the date to the middle or late eighteenth century. But the downward revision is not consistently carried through the book. See the chronological tables, where the XII Egyptian Dynasty is put at 2212–2000 (also 35); the Hyksos invasion at *ca.* 1800 (also 37), with the XIII dynasty occupying all the time between (2000–1750). He begins the I dynasty at *ca.* 3500 (34). Sargon of Akkad is put at *ca.* 2673. And so on.

[4] Y. Kaufmann, *Toledot ha-Emunah ha-Yisra'elit: mime qedem 'ad soph bayit sheni* (*History of the Israelite Religion: From the Beginning to the End of the Second Temple*). (Tel Aviv, 'Dvir' Co. Ltd. 7 Vols. 1937–48.)

[5] M. Noth, *GI*.

[6] We mention the following as samples: H. M. Orlinsky, *Ancient Israel* (London, Oxford University Press, 1954); P. Heinisch, *History of the Old Testament;* English trans. by W. Heidt (Collegeville, Minn. The Liturgical Press, 1952); E. W. K. Mould, *Essentials of Bible History* (New York, The Ronald Press, rev. ed. 1951); Bailey and Kent, *History of the Hebrew Commonwealth* (New York, Chas. Scribner's Sons, rev. ed. 1949); Daniel-Rops, *Sacred History;* English trans. by K. Madge (New York, Longmans, Green & Co., 1949); I. G. Matthews, *The Religious Pilgrimage of Israel* (New York, Harper & Bros. 1947); F. James, *Personalities of the Old Testament* (New York, Chas. Scribner's Sons, 1939); H. W. Robinson, *The History of Israel: Its Facts and Factors* (London, Duckworth, 1938). In addition, W. F. Albright, 'The Biblical Period' (reprinted from *The Jews: Their History, Culture and Religion*, L. Finkelstein, ed. [New York, Harper & Bros. 1949] may be singled out as a splendid stop-gap for students).

[7] I think especially of the works of Albright and Orlinsky just cited. The work of James, while not properly a history of Israel, I have found useful in the orientation of undergraduates to that subject.

acquaintance with current research that they are on no account to be recommended.[1] Still others, of varying merit and differing aim, but reasonably well informed and of a scope suited to classroom use, nevertheless present a picture of Israel's origins, and of the nature and development of her faith, such as leaves one distinctly unhappy.

3

It is manifestly impossible here to review and criticize all these works. In any case, to do so is uncalled for. For it is not our aim to weigh the merits of the various books, but to evaluate the *method* by which the early history of Israel is approached. And, in this regard, in spite of infinite variation in detail, the above books tend to fall into certain general categories—or schools, if you will.

Let it be repeated that, as regards the actual reconstruction of the origins and early history of Israel, and the nature of her religion, no one book is exactly like another. This is advance warning that we cannot make our categories too water-tight without unfairness. We must take care not to 'type' books, and thus to pass glib judgement on them. Some books, in fact, are of such originality that they do not fit well in any type: they are themselves. Nevertheless, whoever is familiar with this literature, and examines the various works for the underlying method of approach to early tradition and history, will begin to detect certain family likenesses even between otherwise quite diverse books. The actual evaluation of tradition, and the actual reconstruction of events, may vary widely—yet the *method* of evaluation may be fundamentally the same.

In fact, I should be prepared to argue that the bulk of the treatments of the history of Israel produced in this generation fall into one of two general classifications as regards our problem—albeit, I repeat, with infinite variation in detail. On the one hand, there are those that approach the problem from the point of view of the classical literary criticism, and reflect more or less faithfully the methods developed in the critical school associated with the name of Wellhausen. On the other hand, there are those that to a greater or lesser degree stand apart from the higher-critical tradition. These last, in most cases, find their evaluation of the early traditions—again to a greater or lesser degree—controlled by a 'high'

---

[1] I refuse to document this statement. To do so would in honour oblige me to a debate with the books in question, which would be beside the point here. I do not necessarily refer in particular to any of the works listed in n.[6] p. 18.

view of biblical inspiration, and a consequent respect for biblical tradition, held in accordance with ecclesiastical dogma or confessional theology, as the case may be.

It is not necessary for our purposes to spend a great deal of time on either of these categories. On the one hand, neither approach is in any essential new: students have long since had ample time to examine, ponder and evaluate, and to draw their own conclusions. On the other hand, neither offers, in my opinion, a consistent and satisfactory answer to the problem of method that concerns us. On the contrary, the two but represent an extension of the battle lines of the nineteenth century—higher criticism versus orthodoxy—in which the very problem with which we are dealing was first raised. And their results underline the unsolved nature of that problem.

I say 'extension' advisedly. For certainly the exact issues are not being contested today that plagued the nineteenth century. There has been considerable realignment of position on both sides. On the one hand, Wellhausenism in its classic form is no longer a live issue. The ranks of the Wellhausen orthodoxy are now sadly depleted by death and desertion and, of those that maintain their faith in the cause, many do so only with severe mental reservations. On the other hand, orthodoxy itself—save in extreme fundamentalist circles—has made concessions to the new learning, rectifying its lines, as it were, by strategic withdrawals here and there, but without compromising its main line of defence. Yet it must be repeated that most of the works of the last twenty-five years carry forward the tradition either of the critical schools or the theological orthodoxy of the last century. In spite of the access of knowledge available to both sides, and in spite of concessions made by both, as regards the method of approach to the early history of Israel, these works represent no *essential* advance over the respective positions of a half-century and more ago.

The historical worth of the early traditions—and therewith the reconstruction of early history and religion—became a problem precisely with the rise of the critical study of the Old Testament, which reached its classical form in the work of Wellhausen and his school. Before that time, to speak in general, orthodoxy had regarded the Bible account in all its parts as inspired of God and inerrant. As for the Pentateuch, it was written by the hand of Moses. It contained, therefore, save for the Genesis narrative, a first-hand account and was, in any case, protected from error by divine inspiration. The whole of it could thus be used with full confidence for the writing of the early history of Israel—and even the biographies of Abraham or Moses—all of which occurred just as the Bible had it. The Wellhausen school, on the contrary, was driven by its methods and presuppositions to a drastically sceptical evaluation of the same narratives.

The methods and results of the Wellhausen school are too well known to require extended discussion or full documentation. This school was characterized first of all, of course, by its meticulous care for literary analysis. It was here that there was developed and perfected that documentary criticism which is still, in its essentials, accepted today. It was insisted that the history of Israel could be written only when the work of analysing the documents of that history—their date, manner of composition, theological tendency, authenticity—had been done. And surely this was right. True, that analysis was often carried to the utmost extremes of verse chopping, and became far too neat, far too subjective a thing to bear the weight that was put upon it. Yet the criticism of the documents remains, in its assured results, an abiding contribution upon which the historian turns his back at his peril. The Wellhausen school was further characterized by a concern for the history of Israel's religion as an organic and developing entity. Indeed, the religion of Israel was placed at the very centre of interest in the writing of her history. And surely this too was right. One need not accept the unilinear evolutionary pattern in which that development was viewed, but one can hardly deny that the religion of Israel developed and adapted itself considerably in the course of history. I shall return later to voice my conviction that a history of Israel which is not in some measure also a history of her faith is neither significant nor possible.

But this very approach led to an extreme scepticism regarding the early history of Israel. It was almost necessarily so. On the one hand, literary criticism increased the distance between the documents and the events of which they told. The oldest of the documents (J) was placed in the ninth century, the latest (P) beyond the exile; nothing in the Hexateuch tradition was thus remotely contemporaneous with the events. On the other hand, there was insufficient appreciation of the fact that much of the material might be considerably older than the document in which it is found: in other words, that to date a document does not necessarily date the origin of its contents. To be sure, the existence of carlier material even in the latest documents was allowed as a possibility by many of the Wellhausen school, but in the practice of history writing this admission was granted very little play. The documents were held valuable for illuminating the beliefs and practices of Israel in the centuries in which they were written; they were not regarded as reliable sources for writing the history of the centuries about which they purport to tell. In other words, the documents were *here*, Israel's origins *there*—and there was no bridge between. Nor were the founders of biblical criticism, because of their presuppositions, willing to hail in a doctrine of inspiration, as it were as a *deus ex machina*, to bridge the gap. The history of Israel was to be written like any other history. The traditions of Israel's origins were cult legends and the like, of late date and minimal historical value. As a result, very little of a positive nature could be said from the side of the Bible concerning the earliest history of Israel at all.

Nor were the founders of biblical criticism able to draw upon a wealth of extra-biblical data to aid in filling the blank. Archaeology and linguistic sciences were then in their infancy; little was known at first hand of the ancient Orient of the second millenium B.C. At the same time, in the absence of an objective frame of reference, and because of certain presuppositions regarding the evolution of man's religion, the familiar developmental pattern was drawn in as a framework upon which to peg Israel's history. The catchwords: polydaemonism—henotheism—monotheism, or fetishism—polytheism—monotheism, or the like, are too well known to require discussion. They became no less than the creedal confession of the critical orthodoxy. All religions, Israel's included, must have developed along these lines. This scheme had its origin, of course, in a Hegelian or a positivist philosophy. But even when the philosophical understructure that supported it no longer commanded acceptance, the tired clichés continued to be repeated faithfully—as some outworn creed is repeated even when the theology that gave it birth is no longer believed or understood. It was first principles that Israel's faith was an evolutionary development from lower forms to higher ones, and that monotheism came late.

But once all this was posited, a drastic reconstruction of Israel's early history followed inevitably. The traditions that tell of the early period are late and in the nature of cult legends and the like. Objective extra-biblical data was meagre. The yawning void was then bridged by the evolutionary framework. And this, *ex hypothesi*, called for a picture of Israel's origins far other than that of the biblical account, with a consequent devaluation of the latter. The patriarchs were customarily denied historical existence, the stories of them relegated to the realm of legend. While Moses was usually allowed to have existed, and an exodus to have taken place, it was held impossible to rely greatly on the Bible traditions in reconstructing the contribution of the one or the details of the other. The conquest narrative of Joshua was regarded as fundamentally unhistorical; the actual coming of the Israelite tribes to Palestine was quite otherwise. But we need not further belabour the matter. Wellhausen's own verdict on the patriarchal narratives is possibly extreme, but thoroughly characteristic: 'It is true, we attain [from the Genesis narrative] to no historical knowledge of the patriarchs, but only of the time when the stories about them arose in the Israelite people; this later age is here unconsciously projected, in its inner and outward features, into hoar antiquity, and is reflected there like a glorified mirage.'[1]

4

But our concern is not to discuss the long-ago work of Wellhausen and his school. The point is that the vast majority of scholarly treatments of the history of Israel down to the present time follow more or less faithfully in this tradition. All the 'standard' histories of Israel in English do so to a greater or lesser degree,[2] while the popular manuals are for the most part saturated with it through and through.

To be sure, one can make such a statement only with qualifications. The books we have in mind by no means exhibit an equal degree of kinship to the Wellhausen tradition: one must resist the temptation to lump, label and cheaply dismiss. Nor must one forget that some of the best scholarly treatments, though based on the methods of critical scholarship, stand so far apart from what is conventionally called Wellhausenism that they do not deserve the label at all.[3] Above all, it must be remembered that orthodox

[1] J. Wellhausen, *Prolegomena to the History of Israel*, English trans. by Black and Menzies (Edinburgh, A. & C. Black, 1885), 318 f.
[2] I refer to the works of Oesterley and Robinson, Lods and Olmstead mentioned in n.[3] on p. 17.
[3] As I shall have occasion to say later, I believe that the work of Kittel (*GVI*) falls in this class.

Wellhausenism has suffered in the course of time so many modifications that it is hard to find it in pure form any longer. A wealth of data, denied to the founders of biblical criticism, is available to the humblest practitioner today. This, plus general loss of confidence in notions of inevitable progress, has conspired to rob the evolutionary pattern of the aura of self-evidence that once surrounded it. Further, what with the progress of form-critical studies, and studies in the history of tradition, there are few today who do not realize that the material in the various documents had a long history behind it, and that documentary analysis is not the end, but only the beginning, of the study of tradition. There have been, we repeat, many modifications. One must at all costs avoid the cowardly sport of whipping dead horses.

Yet if current history books in many details present a different picture from that of a generation ago, it is to be questioned if it is an *essentially* different one. For one thing, the shadow of the developmental pattern still hangs on, though modified in varying degrees, as we have said. This whole category of books has this in common: the religion of Israel is viewed as an evolving entity which progressed upward from lower forms to higher, undergoing a fundamental change of character along the way. Thus the religion of the patriarchs is described as an animism, specifically as a polydaemonism.[1] The god of the Mosaic period is viewed as a tribal god: such epithets as 'mountain god', 'storm god', 'war god', and the like, are used to describe him.[2] On the other hand, the prophets appear as the discoverers of monotheism. And, throughout, the Old Testament is laid under contribution for its developing ideas of God and of ethics.[3]

Furthermore, the approach to the early traditions of Israel is essentially from the point of view of the classical literary criticism. All the books of which we speak base themselves on that criticism, whether through an original analysis of the documents or through

---

[1] e.g. Lods, op. cit., 211–257 among the 'standard' histories; Mould, op. cit., 118–123 among the classroom manuals. There is no need to multiply documentation.

[2] e.g. Lods, op. cit., 308–316; Oesterley and Robinson, op. cit. Vol. I, 88–96; Olmstead, op. cit., 215 f; Mould, op. cit., 130 f; etc.

[3] This is most obviously evident in the popular manuals: e.g. Bailey and Kent, op. cit., 354 f: 'Israel's glory consists in the ideals it gave to the world'; or 188, where it is said that in Amos such notions as 'democracy, brotherhood and the religion of kindness—are clearly heard for the first time in Hebrew'; Mould, op. cit., 315 ff, where the eighth-century prophets are called 'thinkers', and where it is said: 'Amos definitely lifted religion from the ritual to the ethical level'. But the extreme is surely in Matthews, op. cit., where some dozen phases in the development of Israel's faith are isolated and described.

the adoption of its accepted results. This, as we have said, is in itself no demerit, but a positive merit. Yet it means that the problem of the early history of Israel, set up by the rise of higher criticism, remains in full force. While one senses a growing concensus that all the documents, even the latest of them, contain material with a long pre-history of tradition behind it, and a concomitant recognition of the likelihood of a greater historical nucleus in the material than was formerly conceded, one senses equally that this insight is allowed little weight in the actual writing of history. The gap between the situation that gave rise to the traditions, and the finished form of those traditions, remains great and unbridged. Historical reminiscences the traditions may well contain, but who can say with certainty what these are? The historian hesitates to lay weight on the traditions in reconstructing the early history of Israel.[1]

Nor has the new data provided by archaeology, voluminous though it is, been allowed to make any decisive impact on the problem. In the case of works dating from the earlier part of our twenty-five-year period, this may have been in good part because they were written before the more recent discoveries were made, or certainly before there was time for them to be assimilated fully. And for this there can be no blame. In other cases, one fears, there was failure to take into consideration all the data available at the time, or even a shocking ignorance of it.[2] Nevertheless it must be said that the best of the works with which we are concerned show themselves to be aware of the significance of archaeological discovery for writing the beginnings of Israel's history, and make every effort to bring it into the discussion. Certainly these works present a fuller, more chromatic picture of the period than was possible a generation ago. But not an essentially different picture! The new evidence, far from furnishing a corrective to inherited notions of the religion of earliest Israel, tends to be subsumed under the familiar developmental pattern.[3] Nor does it in general alter the essentially sceptical evaluation of the early traditions.[4]

[1] e.g. Lods., op. cit, 152, who likens the effort to reconstruct the patriarchal age from the Genesis traditions to an attempt to reconstruct the age of Jesus from traditions no older than St Louis or Francis I.

[2] Once more, I must beg leave not to document this statement.

[3] So in practically all the histories of the past twenty-five years written from the critical position: e.g. Lods, op. cit., 251–253 who, although making use of a mass of archaeological data, still describes the religion of the pre-Mosaic Hebrews as 'a polydaemonism tinged with polytheism' or a polydaemonism 'moving towards polytheism'.

[4] Lods, op. cit., 151–162; Olmstead, op. cit., 194 f, are good examples.

Thus we see that, as far as the early history of Israel is concerned, the problem remains essentially as it was with the founders of biblical criticism. Nor has there been in these works any essential advance toward a method for attacking the problem. It is agreed that the traditions contain some historical reminiscences. But when it comes to isolating what that is, to separating the genuine historical kernel from the saga form in which it is transmitted, one senses the want of any agreed method. Indeed, one might say that the evaluation of these traditions, aside from a tendency to trust the older documents over the later ones (itself a questionable procedure in the light of what is now known of the history of tradition) seems in the final analysis to be up to the taste and judgement of the individual critic, and the degree of reliance his personal predilections allow him to place on these traditions.[1] The result is that scholars working on the same material, and by the same method—or want of it, vary in their evaluation of the traditions from an almost complete scepticism to a considerable degree of reliance upon their trustworthiness.[2] What raises objection is not so much the details of the various reconstructions in themselves—whether negative or positive—but that none of them seem to have been achieved on the basis of any firm method. The gap between the completed form of the traditions in the Pentateuch documents, and the period to which their narrative relates, must be bridged more or less subjectively. Certainly this is not the school, for all its past contribution and present merits, that will write the history of the future.

5

There remain, however, a number of works produced in the past twenty-five years that stand apart from the Wellhausen tradition and from the classical literary criticism as such. Here one finds both an explicit rejection of the developmental pattern and a far more positive evaluation of Israel's early history and faith than is offered in the works discussed above. Indeed, a rather complete confidence in the historicity of the biblical record is exhibited throughout. The early traditions of Israel tend to be accepted as true historical records, if not literal history. One senses that this

---

[1] Frankly admitted by F. James, op. cit., 3—who accords unusual respect to the traditions. Cf. also the trenchant criticism of M. Noth (*GI*, 39).

[2] This last notably James; see his reconstruction of the career of Moses, op. cit., 1-44.

conservatism *vis à vis* biblical tradition is supported by the doctrine of Scripture which the author in question espouses, and which controls in good measure his evaluation.

Theoretically, one ought to place in this category works from the pen of any who subscribe to a doctrine of full or substantial scriptural inerrancy, or whose evaluation of tradition is in any way controlled by a doctrine of inspiration, however widely these might differ from one another on every conceivable point. Thus works from sources as wide apart as Protestant fundamentalism and the Church of Rome would properly belong here. In practice, however, so far as I know, Protestant fundamentalism has been singularly unproductive of late where history writing is concerned, so that we are actually concerned with works from Roman Catholic sources.[1] Of these there have been several in recent years, including full-length works of reference,[2] works designed for text-book use,[3] as well as popular treatments written for the general reader.[4]

While one fully recognizes the merits of the best of the Roman Catholic works, together with the learning of their authors, it is again unnecessary for our purposes to launch into an extended discussion of them at this point. This is not, let it be repeated, that these works are without value. To the contrary! It is merely that they offer nothing essentially new in their approach to the early traditions of Israel, nor do they make any real contribution to the problem of a method for evaluating them. Indeed, the problem, if raised at all, is rather summarily dealt with.[5] One senses that, for theological reasons, it is not felt as a problem. While it is admitted that the Bible narratives are not inerrant in every detail, and the early traditions not historical annals in any proper sense, they are nevertheless treated as fully trustworthy accounts. To put it otherwise, if a problem is felt, it is resolved out of hand by appeal to presuppositions regarding the reliability of Scripture—

[1] I do not mean to imply that the fundamentalist pen has been dry. On the contrary, there have been a number of manuals of archaeology, introductions to the Old Testament, and the like, all of which set forth an underlying viewpoint as regards the Bible: e.g. E. J. Young, *An Introduction to the Old Testament* (London, Tyndale Press, 1954); Joseph P. Free, *Archaeology and Bible History* (Wheaton, Ill. van Kampen Press, 1950); Merrill F. Unger, *Archaeology and the Old Testament* (Grand Rapids, Zondervan Pub. Co. 1954). But I do not know of any recent, full-length treatment of the history of Israel.

[2] Ricciotti, op. cit. in n.[1] p. 18.

[3] Heinisch, op. cit. in n.[6] p. 18.

[4] e.g. the works of Daniel-Rops op. cit. in n.[6] p. 18.

[5] Cf. Ricciotti, op. cit. Vol. I, 113–125; Heinisch, op. cit., 61–70, on the patriarchal traditions.

and to faith.[1] As a result, the reconstruction of Israel's early history in these books reproduces faithfully the biblical account.

For my own part, I am not among those who are inclined to sneer at a reverence for Scripture, or who lightly pooh-pooh the historicity of its traditions. Furthermore, I must confess that I find the reconstruction of early Israelite history found in these Catholic works in many ways more satisfying than certain extremely negative ones. Yet the feeling cannot be resisted that, right or wrong, the reconstruction has not been achieved on the grounds of sound historical method. The doctrine of Scripture appears as a *deus ex machina* to solve the problem. The problem is thus removed from the sphere of the historian into a realm where the historian as historian may not enter. The assumption is posited, tacitly or explicitly, that the traditions of Israel are not to be evaluated as other traditions are, nor is the history of Israel to be written as other history—but on a higher plane.

The above does not mean, of course, that Roman Catholic writers reject the findings of literary criticism out of hand. On the contrary, one notes that Catholic scholars are allowed surprising freedom in this regard. As Heinisch, for example, points out,[2] the Catholic scholar is required to affirm simply the 'substantial Mosaic authenticity and integrity' of the Pentateuch. Beyond this, a considerable post-Mosaic element may be admitted. One senses as one reads that this last may mean much or little: a few glosses or vast blocks of material. Heinisch, for example, sets the composition both of D and H in the reign of Hezekiah,[3] although holding that both contain earlier material, much of it Mosaic. He thus differs from some of the more conservative critics only in degree. Yet when he comes to reconstruct the work and career of Moses, and the Mosaic faith,[4] so far as I can see all parts of the Pentateuch are drawn upon indiscriminately as a first-hand witness. In short, although literary criticism is used, its consequences are not drawn. The problem of the time gap between the events and the admittedly late redaction of the tradition is not faced, or is not

---

[1] So Ricciotti, op. cit. Vol. I, 121, where he frankly states that the difference between his own and the Wellhausen position is fundamentally one of *a priori* presuppositions in this regard. His own presuppositions (125) oblige him '*de suivre pas à pas le fil de la narration biblique*'. Even more frank is Daniel-Rops, op. cit., 55, who says that the epic of the patriarchs 'is presented to us in the Holy Scriptures as a page of history, and it is a matter of faith for Christians to accept this text'.

[2] Heinisch, op. cit., 448, n. 78.

[3] Heinisch, op. cit., 250, 260 ff.

[4] Heinisch, op. cit., 76–119.

felt as a problem. The gap is bridged by recourse to a doctrine of Scripture.

As for the new light shed by archaeological research, Roman Catholics—like conservatives generally—tend to welcome it gladly for the support it brings to the Bible story. To be sure, the amount of such data actually brought into the discussion in Catholic works will vary, as it will in works from other sources, with the scope and aim of the work in question, and with the competence of the author. But, in general, it can be said that Catholic writers are thoroughly conversant with this material, and use it generously. Yet one cannot help sensing that this use tends to be selective. Not in a quantitative sense merely—for a quantitative selection is of course necessary, so massive is the evidence available. What is meant is that archaeological evidence is brought in as a support to the biblical narrative, while evidence that adds to the complexity of the problem tends to be ignored.[1] In other words, archaeological evidence is not allowed play as an effective control on the biblical tradition, but is used rather as an apologetic tool to bolster up its historical accuracy.

Finally, it must be said that works of this category frequently tend to write the early history of Israel in such a way that history and theology become confused. If the higher-critical schools wrote a history of religion, orthodoxy tends to write theological history. Thus, for example, Heinisch[2] frankly states that he is writing 'to indicate the steps taken by God to prepare mankind for the appearance of the Redeemer'. Thus, too, throughout his treatment of the early history, God appears as an actor in the events, calling Abraham, granting a revelation to Jacob, and the like.[3] Now there is something laudable in this concern for theology, and I confess that I find it more to my liking than the arid objectivity of certain critical works. Furthermore, in certain didactic situations such an approach may be fully justified. Still further, I am not among those who feel that the historian, out of devotion to some sacred cow of objectivity, is forbidden to inject his own theological convictions into his work, provided he does so at the right times and in the right way. But history and theology must be

---

[1] As an example, cf. the handling of the problems of Jericho and Ai in Heinisch, op. cit., 83, 129f; cf. also my review of Heinisch in *JBL*, LXXII (1953) 265 f. It must be stressed that this tendency is by no means confined to Roman Catholic works, but is equally observable in Protestant works of fundamentalist character; cf. my review of Free, op. cit. in *Interpretation*, IV (1950), 496.

[2] Heinisch, op. cit., 3

[3] Cf. Heinisch, op. cit., 52–60; Ricciotti, op. cit. Vol. I, 128, 135, etc.

kept separate lest both historical event and theological interpretation of that event be placed on the same plane. If these two are
confused, the historian will begin to write history, as it were, from
the side of God, and God himself will tend to become a datum of
history.

This confusion is at all costs to be avoided. Abraham is a datum
of history, and the theology of the Yahwist is likewise a datum of
history: both are to be evaluated as such at the proper place.
Furthermore, the historian as a believing man may concur with
the Yahwist that God did indeed act to call the people Israel into
being; and, if so, it is not against the rules for him to say as much.
Faith may affirm that God is the prime actor in Old Testament
history; but he is not a datum of that history within the control of
the historian as Abraham, or Moses, or the Yahwist are. The
actual course of the events, the Old Testament's theological interpretation of those events, and the historian's own faith in God,
must be kept sharply separate lest confusion result. Failure to do
this can only be accounted a weakness of method.[1]

6

But we need dwell on these things no longer. The above
approaches to the history of Israel have long been before us; the
necessary has been said concerning them over and over again. We
shall devote the bulk of our study to certain of the works already
listed which stand sharply out of the two categories that we have
been discussing, and which represent fresh approaches to the
problem.

Now the problem of writing the early history of Israel is, as we
have said, aside from that of assimilating and sifting the archaeological evidence in order to reconstruct the background of the
period, essentially one of finding a sound method for evaluating
the traditions, so that one may determine with some assurance
what historical elements—if any—they contain, and thus the
degree to which they may be used in telling the story of Israel's
origins. Or, to put it otherwise, it is a problem of establishing an
objective procedure for bridging the gap between the traditions
in their present form—admittedly relatively late—and the events
and situations that first gave rise to them. It is a problem—so it

[1] Cf. R. H. Pfeiffer, 'Facts and Faith in Biblical History', *JBL*, LXX (1951), 1–14.
One need not agree with all of Pfeiffer's observations in order to sense that he has put
his finger on a most important point of method.

has been argued—to which the historiography of the past has brought no satisfying or consistent solution.

It is not to be supposed, however, that this unsatisfactory state of affairs has not been seen for what it is, or that the problem has been given up as hopeless. On the contrary, the past few years have witnessed certain novel and extremely significant attacks upon it which require the most earnest critical evaluation. Two in particular stand out.[1]

The first of these is a method developed in the school of Albrecht Alt and embodied in the works particularly of Alt himself and of his distinguished pupil, Martin Noth.[2] Whatever one thinks of this method and its results, it represents without question the most important and creative school of history writing at work today—at least if one may judge by its prolific output, weighty scholarship, and wide influence. No one may treat the early history of Israel with good conscience without first making critical evaluation of it. It bases itself on the assured results of literary criticism and a rigid application of the methods of form criticism, and issues in a meticulous concern to trace the history of the traditions before they found their present form in the Pentateuch documents. The gap between the traditions in final form and the events that gave rise to them is bridged by means of tradition-history. This school can also boast of a thorough acquaintance with the archaeological data, which are used, it must be said, with often singularly negative results.

The second of these approaches is that developed by Yehezkel Kaufmann.[3] Since Kaufmann is an Israeli who writes almost exclusively in Hebrew, his work is far less well known than the foregoing. Indeed, his influence in international circles has probably been decidedly limited. Nevertheless, because in Jewish circles he can boast of a group of ardent admirers,[4] and because he brings to the problem with which we are concerned an approach of decided freshness and originality—and not a little brilliance—he must be given considered evaluation. Further, since he takes his start precisely from a fundamental disagreement with Alt and Noth, and

---

[1] Again let it be made clear that we do not propose to discuss all the numerous detailed treatments of particular points bearing upon early Israel's history and traditions. We confine ourselves to works that proceed from conscious method and issue in a systematic attempt to write history on the basis of it.

[2] Bibliography in Chapter II.

[3] Bibliography in Chapter III.

[4] I am told by certain of his students that no less a scholar than H. L. Ginsberg has been profoundly influenced by him.

since he is at the same time critical both of the conventional results of literary criticism and of those who would abandon literary criticism altogether, he is doubly interesting. One might say that the gap between finished tradition and event is bridged by a novel literary criticism which has the effect of moving the material of the documents back toward the events.

It is possible that there are other approaches at work on the problem which deserve discussion. For example, were a systematic attack on the early history of Israel to be made from the point of view of the Uppsala school—or of other circles in which oral tradition is stressed—it would certainly need a category of its own. But such has, to the best of my knowledge, not been attempted. If it has, it exists in one of the Scandinavian languages, or has otherwise escaped my attention.

But it might be to the point to ask in this connexion if, granting the presuppositions of the oral tradition school, a treatment of the history of early Israel based on objective method has not been rendered impossible.[1] If I understand correctly, it is held by this school that the substance of the Pentateuch, save for much of the legal material, was transmitted largely in oral form until the exilic and post-exilic period, when it was gradually fixed in writing. In place of the conventional documents: *J, E, D* and *P*, we have a 'P-work' in Genesis–Numbers, and a 'D-work' in Deuteronomy–Kings. *D* and *P* are not documents, but stand for the traditionary circles that brought their respective works to final form. Within the 'P-work', material corresponding to *J* and *E* may be isolated. But, again, we do not have to do with documents, but at most with strata of tradition already so fused in oral transmission that to separate them is impossible. The oral-tradition approach thus represents, at least in its extreme form,[2] an explicit rejection of the methods of literary criticism as such.

It is not our purpose to offer a critique of this approach. The point is that, if we grant its assumptions to be true, in place of the conventional and approximately dateable documents, we are left with two vast traditionary blocks, each containing a mass of un-

[1] A full bibliography of the Uppsala school would be beside the point here. For an introduction, cf. G. W. Anderson, 'Some Aspects of the Uppsala School of Old Testament Study', *HTR*, XLIII (1950), 239–256; E. Nielsen, *Oral Tradition* (London, S.C.M. Press, 1954); also the summary and criticisms of C. R. North in *The Old Testament and Modern Study*, H. H. Rowley, ed. (Oxford, Clarendon Press, 1951), 61–82.

[2] There is, however, a considerable difference of opinion among the practitioners of this approach on this point; cf. the article of Anderson cited above.

differentiated traditions both early and late, which it is impossible to range in any chronological order. But if this be the case, then it would seem that the problem of reconstructing the early history of Israel is immensely aggravated, if not rendered impossible of solution altogether.[1] For all that we can know of this history is what is given to us in the final, fixed form of the tradition—and this dates from the exile and beyond. Nor would there seem to be any sure method for going behind this fixed form of the tradition. By what criteria can one separate early from late in this mass of material? And if one cannot do this, what foundation can there be for an objective writing of history at all? One wonders if under these conditions a real history of Israel is possible, or if the history of Israel will not have to give way to a more or less flat-surface phenomenological description of her life and culture.[2] I raise this merely as a question. I should sincerely like to know the answer. If some objective methodology for dealing with the early history of Israel has been developed in this school, the nature of which has escaped me, I should be happy to stand corrected.[3]

Aside from the Uppsala school and its congeners, there are doubtless other methods of approach to the history of Israel that defy the categories we have set up and demand a classification of their own. As I have indicated above, I feel that the work of R. Kittel,[4] while based in the methods of classical literary criticism, nevertheless stands so far apart from conventional Wellhausenism that it cannot be classified under that head. Its method, taking into consideration the state of knowledge of its day, is a model of sobriety. The works of Albright, too,[5] certainly fall into none of the above categories. If no extended discussion of Albright's method is given, it is because the conclusions of this study represent a fundamental endorsement of it.

[1] C. R. North, op. cit., 76 f, has ably made this same point.
[2] Cf. the remarks of North (op. cit., 77) concerning the *opus magnum* of J. Pedersen, *Israel: Its Life and Culture* (London, Oxford University Press, Vols. I and II, 1926; Vols. III and IV, 1940). Pedersen may be regarded as a precursor of the Uppsala School.
[3] The recent work of E. Nielsen (*Shechem: A Traditio-Historical Investigation* [Copenhagen, G.E.C. Gad 1955]) reached my hands while the present study was in proof. I regret that it cannot be brought into the discussion here. It is possible that it may supply a partial answer to the question of methodology just raised. But I must say that, in my own mind at least, the question still remains.
[4] Cf. n[2], p. 17 and n.[3], p. 23.
[5] Cf. n.[1], p. 17 and n.[5], p. 18.

CHAPTER TWO

THE SCHOOL OF ALT AND NOTH

A Summary

LET us turn, then, to the method of approach to the history and traditions of early Israel that has been developed in the school of Albrecht Alt. It would be well if, at the risk of intruding upon the patience of the reader already familiar with this method and its results, we were first of all to outline, as succinctly as possible consistent with fairness, its salient features. Only so can the subject be set up clearly for our discussion. We shall, therefore, in this chapter content ourselves with an objective delineation. Certain points that arouse question will be indicated as we proceed, but detailed discussion and criticism will be reserved until later.

Our discussion will be based at first hand on the works of Alt and Noth. The cream of Alt's important papers and monographs have now been conveniently collected in his *Kleine Schriften zur Geschichte des Volkes Israel*,[1] and will be referred to as occasion demands. Articles of Noth, almost equally numerous, will likewise be mentioned as there is occasion to do so. We shall be particularly concerned, however, with the methods of the Alt school as they have been applied by Noth, and as they have issued in a systematic attempt to write the history of Israel. More particularly, we shall be concerned with Noth's *Geschichte Israels*,[2] and with his *Überlieferungsgeschichte des Pentateuchs*[3] which laid the critical basis for it. The ensuing discussion will be pegged upon these two works with others drawn in as necessary.

I

Noth's procedure in writing the history of Israel is set forth with admirable clarity, and may be easily grasped, in the opening chapters of *GI*. Before proceeding to that, however, the general

---

[1] Hereafter to be referred to as *KS*.
[2] Hereafter to be referred to as *GI*.
[3] Hereafter to be referred to as *UG*. Noth's equally important *Überlieferungsgeschichtliche Studien I* (Halle, M. Niemeyer, 1943) will be of less concern to us here.

observation should be made that Noth confines himself almost
exclusively to the political and institutional history of Israel: the
nature and development of Israel's faith is brought in only inci-
dentally. Thus, for example, the prophets are referred to only for
the information that their books give of an historical nature.[1] On
the other hand, if one turns back to the discussion of the early
period, one will find that, while a chapter is devoted to the insti-
tutions of the Tribal League, including its cult, the theological
content of early Israel's faith is scarcely discussed at all.

Now it would be unfair to criticize Noth for this as such. Not
only is his book of limited size, it is one of the *Göttinger Theolo-
gische Lehrbücher*, and thus intentionally of limited scope. Other
text-books of the same series are supposed to be used to supplement it.[2] Yet it does give us the right to ask if this is not a serious
lack in any history of Israel. Was not faith too central a moving
force in Israel's history, even in political events, for it to be relegated to the fringes of the picture without throwing the picture
out of proportion? Be that as it may, Noth's book is given a
certain 'bare bones' effect which one may well find distinctly un-
satisfying. As regards the handling of the faith of early Israel, the
suspicion haunts one that there are deeper reasons in play than
mere problems of scope. Is Noth, once he has viewed Israel's
early traditions (as we shall see) with consummate scepticism,
once he has reduced the figure of Moses to the vanishing point,
simply not in a position to make positive statements regarding
early Israel's faith? I ask this as a question. If the question is un-
fairly put, I herewith tender apologies.

1. But to turn to Noth's procedure. In *GI*, 1–7 he seeks to define
what is meant by 'Israel', and so to determine the scope of a history of that entity. This one may find both abundantly clear, singularly illuminating—and highly controversial.

Noth first of all (*GI*, 1–3) makes certain observations with which
we would all agree: that Israel was a historic entity and is, as such,
a fit subject for a history; that this history is to be written like that
of any other nation, and by the same methods; that if there is much
in Israel's history that remains inexplicable, that is no more than is

---

[1] So with Amos (*GI*, 216), Hosea (*GI*, 200 f, 214) and Isaiah (*GI*, 224, 228, 230);
Micah gets a reference in a footnote (*GI*, 189), as does Nahum (*GI*, 234); Habakkuk is
mentioned only in connexion with Duhm's theory relating the prophecy to the days
of Alexander the Great (*GI*, 300). And so on.

[2] e.g. A. Weiser, *Einleitung in das Alte Testament* (Göttingen, Vandenhoeck &
Ruprecht, 2nd ed. 1949).

true of other peoples. Furthermore, place must be left for the activity of God in history if he is not to be reduced to a mere 'first cause' (*prōton kinoun*.) Finally, Noth argues that, although Israel is to be studied in the light of her environment, she remains 'a stranger in this world of hers', the like of which is simply not found elsewhere in human history. True! And this lays upon the historian the obligation to say wherein this is so. We shall ask later whether Noth succeeds in this regard.

Noth then proceeds to a definition of the term 'Israel' (*GI*, 3 f). Aside from certain later, and historically conditioned, uses of the name (e.g. for the Israelite state as a whole, for the Northern Kingdom), the Old Testament employs it only as a designation for a definite group of twelve clans and their eponymous ancestor. The name, to be sure, is of an old type and may have applied to a smaller group before the Twelve-Clan League arose, but of this we have no historical information. For example, the Marniptah Stele of the late thirteenth century mentions 'Israel', but we do not know what group is included under that term. The oldest reference surely known to us for the term 'Israel' is the Twelve-Clan League and this is, therefore, the proper subject of a history of Israel. But, Noth goes on to say (*GI*, 5 f,) since the Twelve-Clan League only began its existence after the settlement in Palestine, the history of Israel can properly begin only at that point. Before that no history of Israel is possible, for before that there was no entity Israel—at least none that one may take hold of. Nor do we know anything definite concerning the pre-history of Israel; all that we have are traditions of the later Twelve-Clan League which, in their present form, presuppose the existence of that League, and thus of Israel.[1] We shall have many questions to ask Noth about this later.

Noth takes a bit of time (*GI*, 4 f) to ask what sort of an entity this historic 'Israel' was. The Old Testament, of course, speaks of Israel as a 'people'. In Noth's opinion there are three marks that distinguish a 'people', and by these there is some justification for so designating Israel. First, *common language*: and this Israel had although, it being a Canaanite dialect, she shared it with many of her neighbours, while her ancestors had no doubt spoken a dialect of old Aramaic. Second, *common homeland* in a definite area: and this,

---

[1] *GI*, 5f: '*Über das geschichtliche Werden "Israels" haben wir keinerlei Nachrichten mehr, sondern nur noch Traditionen über Geschehnisse der Vorgeschichte, die—in der vorliegenden Form schon das nachmalige geschichtliche "Israel" voraussetzen.*'

too, Israel had through most of her history although, to be sure, she never had her land to herself alone. Finally, a *common historical experience*: and, by and large, the Israelite people had this. Yet it is just here that Noth questions the designation 'people'. Israel, he says, had a common historical experience only with severe limitations. In fact, only under Saul, strictly speaking, did she ever approximate it. Before that time the clans, though bound together, seldom acted together. The Davidic state, on the other hand, was not based exclusively on the Twelve-Clan League by any means; and after its fall there were two states which went their separate ways and had different historical experiences. Noth, therefore, concludes that while one may speak of 'the people Israel' for the sake of convenience, one must realize that one means something different from the usual by it. Indeed, one would do better to eschew the term and simply speak of 'Israel'. Here, too, we shall have some searching questions to ask Noth later.

2. We shall not dwell on Noth's justification of the *terminus ad quem* of his work (*GI*, 6 f), for it is in itself unobjectionable and beside the point with which we are presently concerned. Suffice it to say that he carries the story on to the Jewish wars of A.D. 66–70 and 132–5.[1] We shall pass over, too, very useful chapters describing the land of Palestine (*GI*. 7–15) and the world situation down to *ca.* 1200 B.C. (*GI*, 16–36), plus a general discussion of the sources of the history of Israel (*GI*, 36–44), and come next to Noth's treatment of the rise of the Twelve-Clan League of Israel.

Noth begins by sketching the areas in which the various clans settled (*GI*, 45–58). This is very useful indeed, and is based upon the extensive and constructive work that both Alt and Noth have done on the tribal border lists in the book of Joshua.[2] There is no need to review it here. At the beginning of the chapter, however, a most significant statement is made which will be reaffirmed *passim* throughout the book, and which will require detailed

---

[1] I shall not criticize this *terminus*, for it certainly represents a major turning point in the history of Judaism. Where to bring a history of Israel to a close has always been a debatable question; whatever point is selected, it seems to me, must needs be somewhat arbitrary. For my part, I should shrink from going on to A.D. 135 because I could omit the rise of Christianity only with bad conscience, yet to put it in would balloon the subject beyond all reason.

[2] In particular, A. Alt, 'Das System der Stammesgrenzen im Buche Josua', *Sellin-Festschrift* (Leipzig, A. Deichert, 1927), 13–24; reprinted in *KS* I, 193–202; M. Noth, 'Studien zu den historisch-geographischen Dokumenten des Josuabuches', *ZDPV*, LVIII (1935), 185–255. The results of these and other studies are distilled in M. Noth, *Das Buch Josua* (Handbuch zum Alten Testament [Tubingen, J. C. B. Mohr, 1938]).

questioning later. Having already declared that the Twelve-Clan League arose only in Palestine, Noth now goes a step further and asserts that the individual clans themselves took fixed form only on the soil of the Promised Land.[1] They both gained their names and emerged as historical entities in and after the settlement.

This Noth argues (*GI*, 47 ff) in good part on the basis of the names of certain of these clans. While some of them are personal names (in the case of Gad and Asher perhaps divine names), and so can prove nothing to the point, some are such that they could have been gained only in Palestine. Thus the clans themselves could have been formed only then. He singles out Judah (*GI*, 47 f), which, he says, took its name from the mountain spine south of Jerusalem known as *har yehudah* (i.e. they were the people of Mt Judah); Ephraim (*GI*, 51), whose name is derived from the area around Baal Hazor called *har 'efrayim* (i.e. the people of Mt Ephraim); Benjamin (*GI*, 53), whose name means 'those living to the south', and refers to the position of that tribe with relation to those of central Palestine—and hence could have been gained only after arrival in that locality;[2] Issachar (*GI*, 56), whose name means 'hired man' and is to be explained in the light of the servile condition in which that tribe found itself in the land (Gen. 49.15); Naphtali (*GI*, 56 f), which took its name from *har naftāli* ('Mt Naphtali', Josh. 20.7). Here are clans, says Noth, which clearly got their names after their settlement and must, therefore, have been constituted then.[3] The presumption is that all were similarly constituted.[4] Noth concludes, therefore, that the Old Testament traditions are quite wide of the mark not only in giving the Twelve-Clan League existence prior to the settlement, but also in allowing such existence to the individual clans themselves.[5]

We do not need to pause long on the actual reconstruction of the settlement of the clans, to which Noth next turns (*GI*, 58–73). It is the picture already familiar to us from Noth's commentary

---

[1] '—*haben sich erst im Zuge ihrer Landnahme zu festen und bleibenden geschichtlichen Grössen konsolidiert*' (*GI*, p. 45).

[2] He denies that it can be deduced from Gen. 35.16–20 that Benjamin diverged from Joseph in Palestine; *GI*, 64, n. [2].

[3] '*Diese Stämme können ihre Namen also erst auf dem Boden Palästinas erhalten haben; und das bedeutet, dass sie sich erst auf diesem Boden endgültig konstituiert haben.*' (*GI*, 62).

[4] '*Dasselbe wird dann aber auch für diejenigen Stämme anzunehmen sein, aus deren Namen nichts Entsprechendes erschlossen werden kann*' (ibid).

[5] '*Die alttestamentliche Überlieferung geht also nicht nur darin über den wirklichen Tatbestand hinaus, dass sie die Namen der Stämme weit über die Zeit der Landnahme hinaus zurückreichen lässt, sondern auch darin, dass sie die Stämme selbst als längst vorher gegebene Grösse behandelt.*' (ibid).

on Joshua, and from the writings of Alt.[1] In a nutshell, the conquest represented no great military action but (*GI*, 59) 'was for
the most part carried out in a rather quiet and peaceful manner'.
It was a long process, beginning as semi-nomad clans pressed into
unoccupied areas in the mountains, in between the holdings of the
city states, in search of summer pasture for their flocks. Then, after
perhaps many years of this, for various reasons, one clan after
another transferred its base from the steppes to the towns and began to settle down. So far all was, with few exceptions, peaceful.
It was only after the clans were already settled, and had begun to
exert pressure on the city states on their borders, that instances of
warlike encounter began to occur. But these were, in any event,
not numerous, and represented only the *final phase* in the long
process of settlement.

This means, of course, that the tradition of a unified onslaught
as given in Josh. 1–12 is unhistorical. The traditions of Josh. 1–9
refer not to 'all Israel' but only to Benjamin (Ch. 10.1–15 is an
Ephraimite tradition, Ch. 11 Galilean), and the figure of Joshua
had no original place in them.[2] Josh. 1–9 consists of a row of
aetiological tales (*GI*, 63), without original connexion to one
another, or to Joshua, and without historical value. They were
drawn together under the presupposition that Benjamin once
fought its way in from the east.[3] They constituted originally the
conquest tradition of Benjamin; and no doubt each tribe had had
its own similar tradition. It was only when, with the formation of
the Twelve-Clan League, there emerged the idea of 'all Israel',
that, for reasons Noth does not adequately explain (*GI*, 63 f),[4] the
Benjamite tradition became the 'all Israel' tradition, suppressed
most of the others and was subsumed under the hero Joshua.

The actual events, as Noth reconstructs them (*GI*, 64–69), were
far more complex—and quite other—than the story of Josh. 1–12.
Benjamin made its way in from the east; Joseph did likewise, with
Gad a part of the same movement but lagging behind in Transjordan (Gilead was a later back-movement of Ephraim to the east,

---

[1] Noth, *Das Buch Josua*, op. cit. in n.[2] p. 37,; Alt, *Josua* (*BZAW*, 66 [1936], 13–29;
reprinted in *KS* I, 176–192); *idem*, 'Erwägungen über die Landnahme der Israeliten
in Palästina', *PJB*, 35 (1939), 8–63; reprinted in *KS* I, 126–175, etc.

[2] Alt, *Josua*, op. cit. in n.[1] finds Joshua original only in 10.1–15, 17.14ff and
Ch. 24; elsewhere he is secondary.

[3] '—ätiologischen Erzählungen, die zusammengefasst sind auf Grund der Voraussetzung,
dass der Stamm Benjamin einmal vom Osten her—eingerückt sei' (*GI*, 63).

[4] In *Das Buch Josua*, op. cit. in n.[2] p. 37, xi, Noth explains this by reference to the
enormous prestige of the shrine of Gilgal, presumably the *Haftpunkt* of the Benjamite traditions, in the days of Saul and later.

as was Machir of Manasseh: *GI*, 52). At an earlier stage, Simeon and Levi had briefly occupied the Shechem area, but had been thrown out (Gen. 34; 49.5–7)—Levi to be scattered, Simeon to fall back into the Negeb. Reuben, too (Josh.15.16; 18.17), had once had foothold west of Jordan and (*GI*, 54 f) was still there in the days of Deborah (Judg. 5.15b–16), but was subsequently displaced. The south, meanwhile, had been settled by clans moving in from the Negeb: Caleb, Othniel, the Kenites, etc., together with Simeon. Judah, on the contrary (*GI*, 66), had probably come in from the east in the first phase of Israelite occupation. Zebulun and Issachar—as is argued by their connexion with Leah—had probably once settled in central Palestine along with Reuben, Simeon, Levi and Judah, but had then pushed to the north, where Issachar fell foul of unfortunate circumstances and got his name 'hired man' (*GI*, 67 f). And so on. As for dates, the beginnings of this process must lie in the latter half of the fourteenth century (*GI*, 70), the end probably by the thirteenth century, certainly by the twelfth.

This is not the place to pause for an evaluation. Yet one cannot refrain from risking the question if there is not some inconsistency in all this. For if, as Noth has argued above, the clans took shape and even gained their names *after* their settlement, it would seem that one ought not to discuss their migration *as clans* prior to that time at all. Before the settlement there would have been, *ex hypothesi*, only the various components of the later clans—who did not even wear the names of those clans—and these presumably could have arrived at various times and from various directions. But that is a question to which we shall return later.

2

But now that, one way or another, we have gotten the Israelite clans settled in Palestine, we shall skip Noth's chapter (*GI*, 74–95) on the constitution of the Amphictyony,[1] and proceed to inquire what he has to say about the traditions of Israel concerning her earlier period. And here, agree with Noth or not, one must admit that he is thoroughly consistent. Having begun the history of Israel with the emergence of the Twelve-Clan League in Palestine —before that time there was no Israel, and so no history of Israel

---

[1] Noth, *Das System der zwölf Stämme Israels* (Stuttgart, W. Kohlhammer, 1930) is of fundamental importance.

—he refuses to treat the traditions of the patriarchs, the exodus, the wilderness wandering and the conquest in any other light than as the sacred traditions of that Twelve-Clan League.[1] This brings us to the heart of Noth's method of handling early Israel's traditions and, at the risk of boring the reader already familiar with it, it is necessary that we sketch at least its broad outlines. It is briefly treated in *GI*, 96–120; but our chief source at this point is, of course, *UG*.

1. First of all, it should be noted that Noth bases himself on the methods of the classical documentary criticism rigorously carried out. The first forty pages of *UG* are devoted to an extremely closely reasoned analysis of the Pentateuch documents, which one is certain to find most helpful and good. And his conclusions are, in general, those of the 'classic' criticism—as he expressly states (*UG*, 24). With Volz and Rudolph he agrees that *J* is the basic literary material of the Pentateuch, although *P* provides its literary frame. But against Volz and Rudolph he protests the effort to eliminate *E* (*UG*, 21–24): *E* is a separate source, although it now exists in such fragmentary form that it is folly to try to reconstruct it as a continuous document. The *E* material has been used as a supplement to *J* (*UG*, 25).

Noth is equally constructive when he comes (*UG*, 40–44), to evaluate the relationship between *J* and *E*. While he finds them too alike to be independent of one another, he denies that *E* is dependent on *J*, or *J* on *E*. In fact, it cannot be proved that *E* is later than *J*, nor can absolute dates be given for either (*UG*, 40, n.143). The only answer is that both go back to a common source (*Grundlage*) which he designates by the symbol *G*, from which both took the basic elements of their material. Although the broken state of *E* makes full reconstruction of *G* impossible, it may be assumed to underlie wherever *J* and *E* coincide (*UG*, 42).

Here Noth takes issue with von Rad[2] and goes a step beyond him. Von Rad had argued that the main themes of the Hexateuch are already to be found in the ancient Cultic Credo, examples of which may be seen in Deut. 26.5–9; 6.20–24 and Josh. 24.2–13, but that it was the Yahwist who so filled out this basic framework that the Pentateuch was given its definitive form. The Yahwist, said von Rad, was responsible for three major additions: working

---

[1] '*Wir können sie daher geschichtlich nur fassen als die Überlieferungen der im Kulturland vereinten Stämme über die entscheidenden Grundlagen ihres Glaubens*' (*GI*, 97).

[2] G. von Rad, *Das formgeschichtliche Problem des Hexateuchs* (Giessen, 1938). I have never been able to secure a copy of this book, so know it only at secondhand.

in the Sinai tradition ('*Einbau der Sinaitradition*'), which is not mentioned in the ancient credos and which had had a separate history; expanding the patriarchal tradition with a host of material available to him ('*Ausbau der Vätertradition*'); adding as a grand introduction the primeval history of Gen. 1–11 ('*Vorbau der Urgeschichte*'). But Noth will not allow the Yahwist so much credit for, says he, except for the last of these, all this is present already in G. To be sure, the Yahwist did fill out the tradition with additional material (e.g. the Hebron-Mamre traditions, the Abraham-Lot traditions), but it is clear 'that the major themes of the Pentateuch narrative were already contained in G and in the order of arrangement which is known to us' (*UG*, 42). This means, further, that 'the all-Israel orientation of the Pentateuch narratives belongs to its basic material (*Grundbestand*)' (*UG*, 45).

All this, it seems to me, is very constructive. If *J* is to be dated in about the tenth century, this means that G, with all the main themes of the Pentateuch already present, and with the 'all Israel' orientation of those themes, was in existence in the period of the Judges. Noth (*UG*, 46–48) would set the *terminus a quo* for the fixation of the Pentateuch tradition in oral or written form at the time when, after the settlement, the Twelve-Clan League emerged. The productive stage of that process was over by the time of the rise of the monarchy.

2. But what of the traditions before they found their way to their normative fixation in the Pentateuch narrative? Here the method of *Überlieferungsgeschichte* (tradition-history) goes into play; for surely these traditions had a long history of transmission behind them!

Now Noth isolates in the Pentateuch *five* major themes (*UG*, 48–67), all of which, he believes, were already present in the *Grundlage* from which *J* and *E* drew. They are as follows: 'Exodus from Egypt' (*Herausführung aus Ägypten*), 'Entrance into the Promised Land' (*Hineinführung in das palästinische Kulturland*), 'Promise to the Patriarchs' (*Verheissung an die Erzväter*), 'Wilderness Wandering' (*Führung in der Wüste*), and 'Revelation on Sinai' (*Offenbarung am Sinai*). It is not necessary to sketch the general content of each of these themes; I think it is fairly obvious in any case. What must be understood is that Noth does not isolate these themes merely in order to facilitate analysis, as one might single out the various themes in a novel or a play, the better to grasp the whole. He means it quite literally: the themes, if I understand him, represent blocks of tradition each with a separate history. They were not (*UG*, 48) put together all at once in order to furnish a framework for the remaining material, but developed separately and were only gradually coupled one to another. The order in which Noth lists them above corresponds, he believes, to their order of priority in the history of tradition.

That questions arise at this point both to right and left goes without saying. True, a good case could be made that the Sinai and patriarchal traditions had a separate history.[1] But is the separation of the others more than a rubric of convenience? And is it really so certain that the Sinai tradition actually had a separate existence? We shall return to these questions later.

3. But let us concede for the moment the validity of the separation of themes and follow Noth's procedure a step farther. For, having isolated the themes, Noth then turns to the task of tracing the tradition-history of each. That is to say, he seeks to trace each theme back to its original element, to determine what that original element was, and to describe the manner in which it was in the course of transmission filled out with additional material. Since it is manifestly impossible to review Noth's treatment of all of the themes, let us select one of them as an example: the patriarchs (*UG*, 58–62, 86–127, etc).

(*a*) The patriarchal traditions, says Noth, developed and were handed down (*UG*, 58f) in Palestine quite independently of the remainder of the Pentateuch. It is probable that at one time each clan had its 'patriarchal traditions', of which we have in the Pentateuch only a small selection. The figures of the patriarchs were revered as the founders of the cults associated with their names: those of the 'God of Abraham', the ' "Fear" of Isaac' (e.g. Gen. 31.42, 53),[2] and the 'Mighty One (Champion) of Jacob' (e.g. Gen. 49.24). As Alt has shown,[3] these cults were of a type widespread among the semi-nomads of the day, and marked by an intimate personal relationship between the god and the members of the clan. The element of promise of land and posterity may be assumed to have been an essential and original element in this

---

[1] On the independence of the Sinai tradition, cf. especially von Rad, op. cit. K. Galling, *Die Erwählungstraditionen Israels*, (*BZAW*, 48 [1928] cf. 26–37) had already stressed the relatively small weight laid upon Sinai in later tradition.

[2] As W. F. Albright (*From the Stone Age to Christianity* [London, Oxford University Press, 1946], 188f, 327) has shown, the word *paḥad*, usually translated 'Fear', ought to be rendered 'Kinsman': hence 'The Kinsman of Isaac'.

[3] Alt, *Der Gott der Väter* (Stuttgart, W. Kohlhammer, 1929; reprinted in *KS* I, 1–78).

type of cult. Then, as the various clans settled down, the cults of the ancestors were transferred to Palestine and carried on in connexion with various local shrines; the patriarchs themselves came to be honoured as the founders of these local cults. Originally, however, the promise of land and seed was not given in Palestine, but out on the desert fringe before the clans had settled. The settlement itself was regarded as the fulfilment of promise—which is precisely the reason why the cults of the ancestors were so revered.

It was because they contained (*UG*, 59) this note of promise that the patriarchal traditions were ultimately linked to the themes of exodus and conquest. This involved far more than a mere addition to the quantity of material contained in the Pentateuch. It meant, as far as the patriarchal stories were concerned, an added stress on the element of promise, with a corresponding loss of the note of fulfilment—which was transferred to the theme 'Entrance into the Promised Land'. At the same time, as the gods of the patriarchs were equated with Yahweh, there was imparted to the entire Pentateuch that historico-theological thread of 'promise-fulfilment' so characteristic of it from beginning to end.

(*b*) Now it is quite certain (*sicher*, *UG*, 60) that the theme of the patriarchs at first treated only of Jacob. The other patriarchs, as we shall see, were secondary developments. For it was Jacob-Israel who was revered as the ancestor of the Twelve-Clan League, and he is the 'wandering Aramean' who, alone of the patriarchs, is celebrated in the ancient Cultic Credo of Deut. 26.5–9. The figure of Jacob is of central Palestinian origin, for he is exclusively associated with the shrines of Shechem and Bethel (and, as we shall see, with Ephraimite 'colonial territory' in Gilead). It was only through the influence of the central shrine of the Twelve-Clan League, and the prestige of the Joseph tribes in that league, that Jacob came to be recognized as the father of all the tribes of Israel (*UG*, 61).

The original element in the Jacob tradition (*UG*, 86–95) is that which relates to Shechem and Bethel. These two shrines are linked by the story of Gen. 35.1–5, which, as Alt has argued,[1] provides the aetiology of a pilgrimage practised in later times between Shechem and Bethel, and which itself possibly goes back (so Noth, *UG*, 87, n. 231) to the transfer of the Ark Shrine from the former place to the latter in the period of the Judges. The original *Haftpunkt* of the Jacob tradition is, therefore (and here we meet

[1] Alt, 'Die Wallfahrt von Sichem nach Bethel'; cf. *KS* I, 79–88.

the stress on the *Ortsgebundenheit* of tradition so characteristic of the Alt-Noth school),[1] the tree shrine of Shechem (*UG*, 88). Bethel is itself a secondary location: Jacob stories wandered there with the transfer of the Ark Shrine, and the new shrine began to suppress the old. For example, the vision of Jacob (Gen. 28.13 f), originally at home in the desert, had first been localized at the tree shrine at Shechem, only subsequently to be moved to Bethel. Jacob's connexion to Bethel is, in fact, rather weak ('*verhältnis-mässig schwach*', *UG*, 92 f). Aside from the above-mentioned stories and the tradition of Rachel's grave in the neighbourhood (Gen. 35.16–20), there is little to link him to that place.

Shechem, then, remains the original locale of Jacob and, even after the move of the shrine to Bethel, traditions of him continued their old '*lokale Beziehung*' to that place (*UG*, 89 f). For example, there is the tradition of his purchase of land there (Gen. 33.19—in Gen. 48.22 it is taken by force, and both are *E*), which no doubt had its basis in the fact that the Israelite tribal league had once owned a plot of land near the shrine, so that they might make ritual preparation for their feasts on land that belonged to them. Here Noth makes a remark entirely characteristic of his view of the aetiological origin of tradition (*UG*, 90): 'This state of affairs easily produced the tradition—' In other words, the fact of Israelite ownership of land near Shechem at a later date was enough to give rise to the story that it was Jacob who first purchased it.

As for Gen. 34, however, in spite of its connexion with Shechem, it has nothing originally to do with Jacob (who is secondary here), but with Simeon and Levi. It reflects the historic fact of an early attempt of those tribes to seize land in central Palestine (cf. Gen. 49.5–7). Then (*UG*, 95), having removed Jacob from its story (he plays '*eine so schwache Rolle*' there), Noth reasons that Gen. 34 reflects a period before Jacob had come to be regarded as the ancestor of all Israel. In fact, he declares that this chapter is 'the only narrative in the Old Testament' that demonstrably roots in the history of the period prior to the settlement of all the clans in Palestine.[2]

---

[1] It is impossible to avoid the use of these German terms, but a word of explanation may be in order. As we shall see below, Alt and Noth lay great stress upon the tenacity with which traditions are supposed to adhere to places (*Ortsgebundenheit*). The *Haftpunkt* of a tradition refers to the place to which that tradition adheres and where it was supposedly handed down.

[2] '*Ja, es ist die einzige Erzählung im Alten Testament, deren Wurzeln für uns noch sichtbar in eine geschichtliche Situation hinabreichen, in der noch nicht alle israelitischen Stämme zur vollen Sesshaftigkeit in Palästina übergegangen waren*' (*UG*, 95.)

(*c*) Aside from the above material we have the great Jacob-Esau-Laban saga cycle (*UG*, 95–111). But this is marked, especially by its 'developed saga style' (*UG*, 96), as a relatively late development in the history of the Jacob tradition. That it has its roots in Transjordan is to be argued from the reminiscence that Jacob was buried there (Gen. 50.10a [J], 11 [E]), for the traditions of a local hero tend to cluster around a grave tradition. While the site of Jacob's grave (Atad, Abel-mizraim) is unknown, the *Haftpunkt* (*UG*, 97) of these traditions is clearly in the vicinity of Mt Gilead, an area settled by an eastward migration of Ephraim. Since this region probably had no sedentary population till these Ephraimites arrived, and since it could not for that reason have had local traditions before that time, it is scarcely possible that the Transjordanian Jacob was original, and was subsequently transferred to Shechem and Bethel. It is far more likely (*UG*, 98) that the Ephraimite settlers brought traditions of the patriarch Jacob with them, and then began to expand those traditions with all sorts of narratives which rose out of the conditions of their life in Transjordan. And, because these eastern Ephraimites kept contact with their kinfolk in central Palestine, it is not surprising that the stories of Transjordanian Jacob should soon have become known in Shechem and Bethel.

The Jacob that emerged out of this new life situation is a figure of a wholly different type (*UG*, 99 f). Where the original patriarch had been a cult founder and a recipient of promise, the new Jacob is 'much "more worldly" ': a clever, crooked fellow. The stories about him are not in the terse, older 'sacral' style, but represent 'a clearly younger type of narration'. The new Jacob is really a personification of the clan in the sense that he is a *type* characteristic of its corporate life. In the course of transmission, however, stories of the eastern Jacob have so been fused with those of the patriarch that they can no longer be separated by literary criticism—but only through the methods of tradition-history.

The stories of the Transjordanian Jacob are developed out of two originally separate themes. The first of these is 'Jacob and Laban' (*UG*, 100–3). Its basis lies in the story of the treaty between the two (Gen. 31.44–32.1), an incident which rests in an historical situation: a stone heap erected to mark the border between the Ephraimite settlers and their Aramean neighbours. If Jacob represents the Gileadite Israelites, Laban represents the Arameans.

Whether Laban (*UG*, 101) was originally the name of an Aramean chief known to the Israelites, of merely a type-figure, cannot be said (Noth always writes it 'Laban', in quotes). The story rose out of the fact that a raiding party from either side, once it had passed the border, got off free. So the story developed of how 'Jacob' had somehow stolen 'Laban's' goods and daughters and gotten over the frontier with them: the typically crooked 'Aramean Laban' is beaten at his own game by 'Jacob' (*UG*, 103).

The other theme is 'Jacob and Esau' (*UG*, 103–8). Here we have the characterization of two brothers who followed different modes of life: i.e. both are types. This material has no specific locale (the stories of the meeting at Mahanaim, and the wrestling at Penuel, are both aetiological and secondary: *UG*, 104). Jacob is here again the type of the eastern Ephraimites. Esau is also a type—but of whom? Not of Edom: Edom is far away and Edomites were not in contact with Gilead. (One takes it that Noth excludes the possibility that Edomites could have wandered this far even in their nomadic period before their settlement in the thirteenth century.) Esau must represent a type that existed in Gilead: i.e. he is the type of the hunters (Gen. 25.27) who roamed the forests of Gilead before the Ephraimites came, as opposed to Jacob, who typifies the Ephraimite herdsman (*UG*, 106 f).

The two themes (*UG*, 108 f) 'Jacob-Laban' and 'Jacob-Esau' were then linked by the artificially contrived motif of the flight of Jacob.[1] In its original form, the stay of Jacob with Laban was short. Therefore the tales of his long service in Laban's house represent a later development of tradition *after* the combination of the two themes. When, finally, all of the traditions of the East-Jordan Jacob were combined with those of the patriarch, they appear as an intermezzo in the life of that worthy: he came from west Palestine and returned thither. To the whole was later added (*UG*, 109 f) the story of how Jacob (this time the patriarch Jacob) begat, by Laban's daughters and their handmaids, the twelve clans of Israel. But this is a late and artificial construction.

(*d*) Jacob, as has been said, was the original figure in the theme 'Promise to the Patriarchs'. The locale of the Jacob stories lay originally in central Palestine; Jacob had no primary connexion whatever with the south (*UG*, 109, n. 289). But there were traditions of many 'patriarchs' current among the clans, of whom two—possibly owing to the growing importance of the southern

---

[1] '*das wohl ad hoc gebildete Erzälungsmotiv der Flucht Jacobs*' (*UG*, 108).

clans in the Twelve-Clan League—found their way into the normative tradition of the Pentateuch as ancestors of all Israel: Abraham and Isaac. But, since Jacob already occupied that position (*UG*, 61 f), the only course was to link Isaac and Abraham ladder-fashion before Jacob in geneological chain: Isaac is made father of Jacob and Esau, Abraham father of Isaac.

Abraham and Isaac were figures of precisely the same type as Jacob; they were founders of clan cults and recipients of promise. The seeming difference in character between these two and Jacob is occasioned solely by the injection of the tales of the Transjordanian Jacob into the tradition of the latter. While Jacob's cult was localized in Shechem, the cults of Abraham and Isaac were perpetuated in the Negeb. The paucity of material about Isaac, and the numerous parallels between him and Abraham, make it evident (*UG*, 112 f) that Abraham has overlaid Isaac in the tradition, and that Isaac is the more primitive figure. The *Haftpunkt* of the latter's cult and traditions is uncertain (*UG*, 116–120). It was not Beersheba or Gerar (Gen. 26), the site of Isaac's summer pasture, but probably the spring of Beer-lahai-roi (Gen. 24.62; 25.11), the location of which is unknown. It is probable that Isaac and Ishmael—himself originally a brother of Isaac and only secondarily the son of Abraham—represent two groups of clans who shared the water of the spring and the cult of El-Roi (Gen. 16.13).

As for Abraham, 'it can scarcely be doubted' (*UG*, 120) that the Hebron-Mamre traditions are secondary, for these are to be found only in *J* and were unknown to *G*. Besides (*UG*, 121), this block of material is characterized by its 'younger, developed saga style'. Nor is the grave tradition of Ch. 23 original (although it represents material much older than *P*), for it presupposes the secondary relocation of Abraham in Mamre. Besides, grave traditions do not belong to the basic material of the patriarch traditions. In fact (*UG*, 125), it was the name Machpelah ('Double Cave') that sparked the thought of a double burial and this was, of course, related to Abraham and Sarah. The basic material *re* Abraham is (*UG*, 122 f) the story of the promise in Gen. 15. Noth is embarrassed because this story is not localized at any shrine, but he concludes that it must have been in the Negeb and, further, that the location was undoubtedly originally present in the narrative.[1]

The traditions of Abraham overlaid and in part suppressed

---

[1] '*zweifellos*' (*UG*, 122), '*sicher*' (*UG*, 123).

those of Isaac, both because Abraham and Isaac were figures of identically the same type, and because the locale to which their traditions attached was essentially the same. After Abraham had been elevated to the position of first ancestor of all Israel, the stories about him were cherished (*UG*, 123 f) at the shrine of the Six-Clan League at Mamre[1] and there, as in the case of the Transjordanian Jacob, all sorts of other local traditions were coupled to him, especially the stories of the destruction of Sodom and Gomorrah, the grave tradition of Ch. 23, and the like, many of these of an aetiological character.

(*e*) In this connexion a glance at the figure of Lot, who, in Noth's view, enters the Pentateuch tradition at this point, would be most illuminating. The Lot stories had a long and complex history of transmission (*UG*, 167–70). The kinship of Lot to Abraham through his father Haran, Abram's brother (Gen. 11. 27–32), is surely not original. In fact, Abraham himself is clearly ('*offenbar*', *UG*, 167) a secondary addition to the Lot stories, which consist of various elements, namely: a narrative at home in Hebron concerning the destruction of the cities of the plain, and various local traditions from east of the Jordan. The 'Haran' in the stories is originally derived from the town Beth-Haran, which is mentioned in Num. 32.36, and which lies in an oasis where the Wadi Hesban debouches into the Jordan valley (the name is Beth-Haram in Josh. 13.27 but, according to Noth, this form is secondary). Haran was certainly ('*gewiss*' *UG*, 168) the name of the god worshipped at the place, but later the name Beth-haran was understood as the home of Haran, a godly man ('*frommer Mann*') who had found refuge there from the great disaster that overwhelmed the plain.

Exactly how Beth-Haran had connexion with Hebron-Mamre where, tradition had it, another '*frommer Mann*' lived who was thought of as the brother of Haran, is not certain. At any rate, tradition recounted how this Haran, brother of the '*frommer Mann*' of Hebron, was the one who escaped the calamity and became the ancestor of all the people who lived in the Dead Sea area—for surely the inhabitants of the area were descendants of the sole survivor of that calamity. The story was told in Hebron how the brother there, who had once taken a more modest portion of land, had come off better than the brother who chose the riches of the plain.

[1] On this, cf. Noth, *Das System der zwölf Stämme Israels* op. cit. in n. 1 p. 40 107 f.

As for Lot, he had originally nothing to do with all this. Originally Lot was the subject of a local tradition, the *Haftpunkt* of which was a cave at Zoar (*UG*, 168 f). This tradition, which included the kernel of Gen. 19.30–38, was carried by caravan traders to Hebron, and so became known there also. Lot thus came to be regarded as the ancestor of the inhabitants of the mountains above Zoar. These were not originally Moab and Ammon, for the aetiology of their names is a later adaptation of the tradition which took place after the arrival of these two peoples on the highlands east of the Dead Sea. Ammon, in any event, lived too far from Zoar to be original in a local tradition of that place. It was in the course of the transmission of this local tradition at Hebron that Lot was brought into connexion with Haran, the ancestor of the people of the plain, as the latter's son, and thus the nephew of the '*frommer Mann*' of Hebron. Later, when Abraham usurped the place of this '*frommer Mann*' in the tradition, Lot appears as the nephew of Abraham. Meanwhile Lot ousted Haran from his position and became himself the leading figure in the tale of Sodom and Gomorrah.

3

We cannot pause to sketch in detail the method of *Überlieferungsgeschichte* any further. Suffice it to say that the other themes of the Pentateuch are treated in a similar manner. And if what has been said is admittedly incomplete, I trust that it has conveyed a fair impression of the method by which this important school of history writing deals with the traditions of early Israel. It is easy to see from the above that the attitude adopted toward the historical worth of these traditions is negative in the extreme. Indeed, it is only when one has grasped the method that Noth pursues, and the evaluation of the traditions to which it leads him, that one is able to understand why he insists on beginning the history of Israel only with the emergence of the Israelite amphictyony after the settlement of the clans on the soil of Palestine. He *must* begin there. For, although the traditions of the earlier history of those clans are both numerous and voluminous, their worth as historical sources is held to be so slight—nay, virtually non-existent—that scarcely a single positive historical statement can be made on the basis of them.

1. As for the patriarchs, Noth does indeed concede that they were not mere eponyms, or mythical figures, or the like, but his-

torical persons. Their distinctive cult of the *theoi patrōoi*, with the element of promise of land and seed, represents an actual phenomenon in the history of religion (cf. *GI*, 107). But, beyond that, little can be said of them. While some of the traditions, to be sure, rest upon historical events (e.g. the affair of Simeon and Levi in Gen. 34), in no sense can they be used as sources of history. The most of them, in fact, represent little more than the free creation of fancy. Even in their broad outlines they are not to be trusted. The tradition, for example, that the ancestors came originally from Upper Mesopotamia rests upon no more than the correct awareness on the part of the Hebrews of their kinship with the Arameans, who subsequently had their centre of gravity in this area (*GI*, 72). The home of Laban originally had its locale in the neighbourhood of Gilead (*UG*, 218, 110 n. 294). Later 'the Land of the Children of the East' was thought to be further to the north (so in Gen. 29.1 [J]). But it was only with the rise of Harran as a caravan city and Aramean centre that the Laban-Jacob stories were transferred thither. Thus the story of the migration of the Hebrew ancestors from Mesopotamia is without historical foundation. And, even though the patriarchs were historical individuals, and their religion an historical phenomenon, their actual existence was spun out not in Palestine at all, but on the desert fringe (*GI*, 107 f). It was only with the transference of their cults to Palestinian shrines that their traditions were also transferred thither, and other traditions began to develop.

Nor are we any better off where the events of the exodus, of Sinai and the wilderness wandering are concerned. The historicity of the enslavement of a group of Hebrews in Egypt cannot be doubted, and Noth connects this with the mention of *'apiru* in the texts of Rameses II and his successors (*GI*, 98 f). Nor can one doubt that historical events lay behind the exodus story, if only because its towering importance in Israelite believing will hardly admit of any other explanation. But beyond that affirmation, and a sketch of the general historical and geographical situation, little can be said. The traditions of Sinai, too, undoubtedly rest on historical events (*GI*, 111): they are 'uninventable' (*unableitbar*). But the nature of these events remains a mystery which cannot be clarified. This is partly because of the long, independent history which these traditions had, quite separate from the others of the Pentateuch. Their *Sitz im Leben* is the regular feast of covenant renewal. The covenant represented the submission of the clans to

Yahweh and the recognition of his rule, but the oldest traditions know nothing of a regularly formulated law. The location of Sinai is, of course, not certain; but the Sinai events had no original connexion with the exodus (*GI*, 115 f). They cannot be located surely in time or place; even their inner content escapes us (*GI*, 116). And, of course, Moses had nothing to do with any of this.

2. Most clearly illustrative of the nihilism of Noth's approach, where the historical value of the tradition is concerned, is his treatment of the figure of Moses (*UG*, 172–91, *GI*, 117 f).

It is unlikely (*UG*, 172) that Moses belongs originally in all the Pentateuch themes—save, of course, that of 'Promise to the Patriarchs'. This is argued from the fact that in the historical recollections of the Old Testament outside the Pentateuch, his name occurs but rarely, and little weight seems to be placed upon him till a later period. His name is missing from the old Cultic Credo of Deut. 26.5–9 (as, one might add, is everyone else's), and its presence in Josh. 24.5 is a later gloss (*UG*, 172, n. 446). Only with the Deuteronomic literature does Moses begin to play a central rôle, and it is here that his function as the great lawgiver began to grow in tradition (*UG*, 173 f). *P* of course placed the entire weight of his narrative on the Sinai events. Few references to Moses are to be found in the Old Testament which do not depend on the Pentateuch narrative.[1] Moses is not, therefore, 'the great link' (*die grosse Klammer*) that ties the Pentateuch themes together (*UG*, 177); indeed, if he were really original in all, it might be that the whole thesis of the Pentateuch themes would fall. But he is not original in all.

Moses' place in the various themes (*UG*, 177) is unequal. He stands loosest of all precisely in the theme 'Revelation on Sinai' (*UG*, 178). Indeed, in its most original element, the covenant meal of Ex. 24.1*, 2*, 9–11 (*E*), Moses had no original part. The twelve nameless elders were the real representatives of the people, and Moses has suppressed them. In like manner, so Noth argues, Moses is equally not original in the theme 'Exodus from Egypt' (*UG*, 178–80). Nor does he belong in the theme 'Wilderness Wandering' or in any of its subsidiary motifs (*UG*, 180–2). Nor is he at home, as some have maintained, in Qadesh—for there is no

---

[1] '*Es zeigt sich, dass ausserhalb der sich entfaltenden Pentateuchtradition und des von ihr ausgehenden Einflusses Mose in der alttestamentlichen Überlieferung keine nennenswerte Rolle spielt——*' (*UG*, 175).

'Qadesh Tradition'. So, after a long argument, the details of which we shall skip, Noth comes (*UG*, p. 186 f) to a grave tradition; and there is no surer index of the original locale of a figure of tradition than a grave tradition.[1] That this grave tradition appears first in *D* and *P* is an accident of redaction, for it is very old. Its original narrative context has been lost, so that we cannot say why it was, in the oldest form of the tradition, that God's anger prevented Moses from entering the Promised Land. Nevertheless it would seem that Moses in some way belongs (*UG*, 187) in the theme 'Entrance into the Promised Land'; he somehow prepared the way for that event but was cut off before it came to pass. His grave was in the neighbourhood of Baal Peor (Deut. 34.6), but its exact location was lost from later memory (*UG*, 188 f).

But (*UG*, 190) does this grave tradition rest on the rôle that Moses played in preparing for the conquest? Quite the reverse! The grave tradition is not a development of the theme 'Entrance into the Promised Land'. On the contrary, Moses, because his grave lay in the way of the advancing Israelites, was drawn into the tradition at this point. The ultimate basis of the Mosaic tradition, then, is a grave where Moses really died and was buried. As Noth admits, that is not much, nor does it go far to explain the subsequent significance of Moses in tradition, but it is all that can be said.[2] Historically Moses probably belongs in the pre-history of the central Palestinian tribes, perhaps as a leader in seasonal migrations. From there he was brought into the theme 'Entrance into the Promised Land', and thence into the other themes of the Pentateuch. He does not belong, therefore, to the kernel of the Pentateuch at all (*UG*, 191) but only to its narrative expansion. Thus it would seem that all we know surely of the historical Moses is *that he died*—which, if one may be pardoned a flippancy, would seem to be a reasonable assumption. It is not surprising to read (*GI*, 118, n. 3) that Noth holds it quite erroneous to refer to Moses as a founder of a religion (*Religionsstifter*), or even to speak of a 'Mosaic religion' at all.

3. So we observe that Noth's method leads him to a mistrust of

---

[1] '*Und eine Grabtradition pflegt auch sonst den sichersten Hinweis darauf zu geben, wo eine bestimmte Überlieferungsgestalt ursprünglich hingehört*' (*UG*, 186).

[2] '*Es spricht veilmehr die Wahrscheinlichkeit dafür, dass wir mit ihr auf das Urgestein eines nicht mehr ableitbaren geschichtlichen Sachverhaltes stossen, mit anderen Worten, dass an der bezeichneten Stelle Mose wirklich gestorben und begraben worden war. Damit ist freilich für die Feststellung der geschichtlichen Rolle und Bedeutung Moses nicht viel gewonnen. Es fehlt uns aber jede Möglichkeit, mehr sicheres darüber zu erfahren*' (*UG*, 190).

the early traditions of Israel which is little short of nihilism. But no one will have failed to notice that an equal mistrust of the possibility of utilizing archaeological evidence is involved. We shall speak on this point later: suffice it here to make note of it.

For example, the manifold correspondences between the patriarchal stories and the customary laws of Nuzi—to say nothing of other evidence from Mesopotamia—is explained by saying that Hurrian elements took part in the Hyksos movement (*GI*, 72) and could well have brought such customs to Canaan, where the Hebrew ancestors could have learned of them.[1] Again (*UG*, 178 f), Moses' Egyptian name is cared for by the observation that, after centuries of Egyptian domination of Palestine, its border lands, and the desert to the south, any one at all could have had an Egyptian name without the trouble of going to Egypt to get it— which last, of course, Moses *ex hypothesi* never did.

Noth's attitude toward the relevance and validity of archaeological evidence, reflected *passim* (e.g. *GI*, 70 f) in his works, is developed at length in his article 'Grundsätzliches zur geschichtlichen Deutung archäologischer Befunde auf dem Boden Palästinas'.[2] Here he directs himself specifically to the problem of the conquest, and to the positive use of archaeological evidence with regard to it made by Albright and others. As we have seen, Noth holds that the biblical tradition of that event in Josh. 1–12 is virtually without historical value, with the result that he can declare that from the side of the Bible we have no reliable account of the fall of Jericho, Ai, Bethel, Lachish, Debir, etc. at all. True, these cities (at least Bethel, Lachish, Debir) seem to have been destroyed during the thirteenth century. But before one rushes to illustrate the Joshua story from this evidence, one should weigh the following points: first, the Israelite conquest was not the only movement afoot at the time; these destructions could, for all we know, be due to the Philistines, or to unknown wars between local city states. Second: the Israelite conquest was not a sudden onslaught anyhow, but a gradual infiltration of a largely peaceful nature. And, finally: since the Israelites settled for the most part in vacant areas and did not dare assault the great Canaanite cities, it is not likely that evidence of the Israelite conquest will be found in the excavation of such places. Whether this represents a wilful

---

[1] Alt, 'Erwägungen über die Landnahme der Israeliten in Palästina', op. cit. *KS* I, 174, had already expressed himself similarly.

[2] *PJB*, 34 (1938), 7–22.

triumph of theory over the weight of evidence, we shall ask later.

In fine, we see that the Alt-Noth school, while marked by brilliance of scholarship and consistency of method, is brought by that very method to a totally negative evaluation of the historical worth of the early traditions of Israel and, at the same time, to a surprising reluctance to call upon the results of archaeology in a measure to fill the void thus created. The result is, it is not too much to say, that the traditions of Israel are swung in the air and deprived of effective objective control, while the history of Israel before the settlement in Palestine is robbed of all content and rendered virtually a blank. Yet, so influential is this school, and so learned its leading practitioners, that it is required that we weigh its methods and results with utmost seriousness.

CHAPTER THREE

YEHEZKEL KAUFMANN

A Summary and Evaluation

BEFORE we proceed to a criticism of the Alt-Noth school and its handling of the early history of Israel, it might be well if we first paused to sketch the position of Yehezkel Kaufmann and, in particular, his approach to some of the same problems. For, not only does Kaufmann exert a great influence, especially among Jewish scholars who have ready access to works in modern Hebrew, his point of departure is precisely a fundamental disagreement with the methods of Alt and Noth, and a sweeping criticism of their results. Perhaps we shall find that he had made the necessary criticisms for us, and has thus relieved us of the necessity of doing so ourselves.

I must say at the outset that I undertake to present the views of Kaufmann with some misgivings and with sincere apologies. For I have not yet studied through his major work, the multi-volume *History of the Israelite Religion*.[1] I must in candour confess that to do so promises to be a long and arduous job, for modern Hebrew does not come easily for me. What will be said here will be based primarily on Kaufmann's translated work, *The Biblical Account of the Conquest of Palestine*.[2] While I realize that this allows us but a restricted view of what Kaufmann has done, I believe it to be an undistorted view. At least we shall be able to see enough of his method to make some evaluation of it.

I

1. Kaufmann, as we have said, establishes the validity of the biblical account by means of a novel literary criticism which has the effect of moving its composition back very close to the events it describes. He begins (*BAC*, 1–4) by taking issue with the pre-

---

[1] Y. Kaufmann, *Toledot ha-Emunah ha-Yisra'elit*, op. cit. Ch., I, n.[7] p. 18.
[2] Hereafter to be referred to as *BAC*.

vailing critical position regarding Joshua and Judges according
to which these books, apart from the Song of Deborah 'contain
no original and authentic information' about the period with
which they deal. This view, he says, is supported by three major
lines of argument: first, that both books are in a Deuteronomic redaction and are, therefore, products of the seventh century;
second, that the picture of the conquest in Joshua is in fundamental contradiction to that of Judg. 1, an earlier and more historical account—though even this is usually held to be a synthesis
from the period of the early monarchy or later; third, that the
stories of Josh. 1–11 and of Judges (here the position of Alt and
Noth) were originally of local significance, many of them legends
of aetiological origin, and were only converted into national sagas
by later redaction. In spite of a tendency to give up the effort to
trace Pentateuch sources through Joshua, and in spite of the work
of such scholars as Alt, Noth and Albright, who have found earlier
material embodied in the sources of Joshua—and of Wright, who
has challenged the exaggeration of the contrasts between Joshua
and Judg. 1—[1] there has been, says Kaufmann, no fundamental
change in the prevailing evaluation of this material.

Kaufmann makes it plain that he has no quarrel with higher
criticism as such (*BAC*, 2 f). He objects to the artificial 'scissors
and paste' method by which it often proceeded, and the elaborate
refinement of source of criticism in which it often issued. But,
while he welcomes the healthy protest against 'the debaucheries of
literary criticism' which has come from the direction of Uppsala
(he quotes Widengren), he feels that baby has been thrown out
with bath. The protest is not against literary criticism itself, but
against the ridiculous application of it according to the rules of
Latin composition. To abandon literary criticism is only to make
matters worse, for the sources were at least something concrete
with which it was possible to work objectively.

Now, says Kaufmann, it is beyond dispute that Joshua and
Judges bear the marks of *D*—and of *P* for that matter. Nor does
he question that the extant book of Deuteronomy belongs to the
time of Josiah. But does this, then, force us to date the composition of Joshua and Judges in that period? Kaufmann proceeds
(*BAC*, 4–7) to argue that it does not. To speak of the Former
Prophets as 'a Deuteronomistic historical work' is ambiguous and

[1] G. E. Wright, 'The Literary and Historical Problem of Joshua 10 and Judges 1',
JNES, V (1946) 105–114.

misleading. There is, as most scholars agree, an early nucleus in Deuteronomy and, in fact, only the legislation regarding *unification of the cult* can be dated to the seventh century. Therefore, says he, the historical philosophy of Deuteronomy 'has no original connection with the idea of the unification of the cult and is older than it' (*BAC*, 4). Thus, to class the Former Prophets as a Deuteronomic history (or histories) does not fix their date in the seventh century: one must ask if one is using the term 'Deuteronomic' in its early or in its late sense.

There is, he says, no mention of cultic unification in the Former Prophets until I Kings 3.2 (except for a gloss in Josh. 9.27). Before this point there is indeed contact in style and viewpoint with *D*—but only with the early *D*. Since there is no mention of unification in Joshua and Judges, it follows (*BAC*, 6) that the Deuteronomic element in these books has no connexion with the seventh century. In fact, the Former Prophets are not a unified composition at all. The presence of the note of unification in Kings proves that that book was compiled after the reign of Josiah; the absence of this note in the three preceding books shows that they date from an earlier period. In Samuel, indeed, there is no trace of Deuteronomic redaction at all. It is otherwise with Joshua and Judges, of course, but even these two were not edited at the same time (p. 7). Nor is Deuteronomy to be linked to the Former Prophets as a single work, as Noth has tried to prove.[1] The Josianic edition of *D* did influence Kings, but that is the end of the matter. The fact that all these books share a common style proves only that all were written in the style of *D*, which was an ancient style. In short, the dates of Joshua and Judges cannot be fixed by style, but by internal evidence only.

2. To this internal evidence Kaufmann then turns. He makes much of the fact (*BAC*, 7) that the latest dateable event mentioned in Joshua is the conquest of Leshem (Laish) by the Danites (Josh. 19.47). Nothing in the book can be demonstrated to reflect a later time. Then, after a summary of the work of Alt and Noth on the boundary and city lists in Joshua,[2] and of Mowinckel's criticisms of their results (*BAC*, 8–13),[3] Kaufmann turns to the thesis of Alt that the city lists of Judah, Benjamin and Dan (Josh.

---

[1] Noth, *Überlieferungsgeschichtliche Studien I* (Halle, M. Niemeyer, 1943).
[2] Cf. especially the works cited in Ch. II, n. [2] p. 37.
[3] S. Mowinckel, *Zur Frage nach dokumentarischen Quellen in Josua* 13–19 (Oslo, J. Dybwad, 1946). He argues, against Alt, that the lists are the work of P; they rest on no documents, but a living tradition.

15.20–63; 18.21–28; 19.40–46) represent the districts of Josiah's expanded kingdom (*BAC*, 13–22).[1] If this be so, he concedes, then we must give in to it: Joshua was compiled after the time of Josiah. But the argument stands or falls on the question of whether the territory of Benjamin-Dan in these lists encroaches on that of Ephraim or not, and thus reflects Josiah's aggressive activity in the north. In an argument which we can only summarize he denies it (*BAC*, 15–19). As for Benjamin, only three of the towns in Josh. 18.21–28 might be argued to be on Ephraimite soil: Jericho, Bethel and Ophrah. But the first two are border points, while the last (et-Tayibeh) is not far away. We have here, therefore, no more than a normal fluctuation and intermingling of population such as takes place on any frontier. As for Dan, the case is not different. Kaufmann denies that the border lists left no place for Dan between Judah and Ephraim (Alt);[2] or that, space having indeed been left, it was originally Benjamin's, the western part being marked off by a recensionist to leave space for Dan (Noth).[3] The list of Josh. 19.40–46 does not coincide with the district 'Ekron' of Josiah's kingdom (Josh. 15.45 f). In any event, a glance at the border lists of Judah (15.5–12) and of Ephraim (16.1–3) will show that they do not coincide: there is space between, and all the Danite cities lie in this area. The fact that no border list exists for Dan is easily enough explained by the fact that the borders of Dan have already been circumscribed by those of its neighbours and, in any case (*BAC*, 17, n. 18), it is far from sure that Josh. 19.40–46 does not contain a border list. On the other hand, one thing is immediately apparent which the author of the lists did *not* know: the actual northern area of Dan. He neither defines its borders nor lists its cities. He lived, therefore, before the days of 'from Dan to Beersheba'.

From all this Kaufmann concludes (*BAC*, 19–22) that the city lists do not reflect the situation of Josiah and, indeed, nothing in the Book of Joshua does. If the city lists reflect Josiah's expansion,

---

[1] A. Alt, 'Judas Gaue unter Josia', *PJB*, 21 (1925), 100–116; reprinted in *KS*, II, 276–288.

[2] Cf. references in *BAC*, 16, especially A. Alt, 'Eine galaläische Ortsliste in Josh. 19', *ZAW*, 45 (1927), 66. In 'Das System der Stammesgrenzen im Buche Josua', op. cit. in Ch. II, n. [2] p. 37, *KS* I, 195, Alt holds that the sea coast is divided between Judah, Ephraim, Manasseh and Asher. The territory of Dan. (Josh. 19.41–46) is held to correspond to the district 'Ekron' of Josiah's kingdom (cf. 'Judas Gaue unter Josia', op. cit. in n. [1] *KS* II, 287).

[3] M. Noth, *Das Buch Josua* (Handbuch zum Alten Testament: Tübingen, J. C. B. Mohr, 1938), 81. Noth likewise holds that the territory of Dan corresponds to the district 'Ekron' (ibid., 93).

why—he asks—do they not include more: for example, cities in
the district of Samaria itself into which, according to II Kings 23.15–
20, Josiah extended his reform? On the other hand, he doubts if
Josiah ever conquered the area of Ekron mentioned in the lists
(Josh. 15.45 f). In any event, the towns given to Benjamin and Dan
were not cut out of an administrative list of Judah, if only because
some of these towns are assigned both to Benjamin or Dan *and*
Judah. This reflects merely the mixed population which existed in
border areas. The fact, further (*BAC*, 24 f), that Jerusalem is referred to as 'Jebus, the same is Jerusalem' in the list of Benjamin
(18.28), as well as the fact that Hebron is still Kiriath-arba (15.54)
and Kiriath-jearim is Kiriath-baal (15.60), certainly gives an
antique flavour to the lists. Would anyone in Josiah's day have
still referred to the capital city as Jebus, and then explained that
that is Jerusalem?

But Kaufmann goes farther. Not only (*BAC*, 24 f) are all the
lists of Joshua early, they go back to the very days of the conquest.
The fact that the author is unable to delineate Dan's actual holding, while describing a territory that that tribe never succeeded in
occupying, points to the essentially utopian character of the lists.
The lists do not reflect the actual holdings of the clans after the
settlement, but represent an *a priori* postulate of what belongs to
each tribe. It reflects an act of national policy, an agreed covenant
of all the tribes that took part in the conquest of the land. The preconceived notion that the union of the tribes was a late accom-
plishment is to be rejected.

We shall omit Kaufmann's detailed discussion of the holdings of
the various tribes (*BAC*, 22 f, 25–36). Suffice it to say that there are
many points here that are interesting and well taken, along with
some that are open to question. The lists for the Galilean tribes
exhibit (*BAC*, 25) a confused mixture of boundary and city lists;
those of the Transjordanian tribes (*BAC*, 26–28) have no boundary
details at all. Especially interesting is his argument (*BAC*, 34 ff) that
both the description of Ephraim's holding, and that of Manasseh's, were originally provided with a full register of cities, just as
is the case with Judah. These lists were excised in the late Judahite
(seventh century) edition because the editor had no interest in
them. Scars of excision may be seen for Ephraim in 16.8 f, for
Manasseh in 17.9 f.

Kaufmann next takes up (*BAC*, 40–46) the list of Levitical cities
in Josh. 21. The chapter, he agrees, is *P*. But it is not to be re-

garded, as Wellhausen did,[1] as an expression of the unrealistic demands of the post-exilic priesthood for a territorial portion. Nor
is it, as Noth would have it,[2] a description of the cities occupied by
Levitical families from outside the autonomous Judah of the Per-
sian period. But he also takes issue with S. Klein,[3] who argued
that the list is a register of the actual Levitical settlements in the
age of David, and with W. F. Albright, who dates the list between
Saul and Solomon and argues that it reflects an ideal programme
for the settlement of priests and Levites.[4] Kaufmann brings arguments (*BAC*, 42–44) to support his contention that the chapter reflects no actual historical situation, but is utopian in character. If
it reflected the actual state of affairs in the days of David, he asks,
how is it that such well-known priestly settlements as Shiloh, Nob,
Bethel, Gilgal, Mizpah, Beersheba, Ramah—to say nothing of
Jerusalem itself—are omitted? Further, the whole programme
stems from *P*'s conception of the functional and geneological
segregation between priests and Levites, and attempts to imple-
ment that in a geographical segregation as well: all the sons of
Aaron are south of the Ephraim-Dan border, all the Levites are
north of it! Surely such a situation never existed in fact, and is
clinching argument for the utopian character of the chapter!
Finally, be it noted that, while cities are allocated from each of the
tribes including Dan, the cities of Dan are all from southern Dan,
which, says Kaufmann, was not the *real* territory of Dan, while
none is from northern Dan, which *was* that tribe's real holding.

The list, therefore, is a utopia (*BAC*, 44–46). But it is not a post-
exilic priestly utopia, but a very early one: it 'could have been put
into words only at *the beginning* of the period of the conquest,
before the shrines and bamoth were established in the settlements
of Israel' (*BAC*, 44). It arose in priestly circles at the time of the
conquest and as a result of the situation of the tribe of Levi then.
This tribe had guarded the Tent in the wilderness, but now the

[1] See reference in *BAC*, 40, n. 42. Page numbers differ in various editions of Wellhausen's work: cf. *Geschichte Israels I* (Berlin, G. Reimer, 1878), 164–174.
[2] M. Noth, *Das Buch Josua* (op. cit. in n. [3] p. 39), 100 f.
[3] S. Klein, 'arê ha-Kohanim we-ha-Lewiyyim we- 'arê ha-Miqlat.' ('Cities of the
Priests and Levites and the Cities of Refuge', *Qebets ha-Ḥaburah ha- 'Ibrit lehaqrit
Erets Israel wa- 'atiqoteha*, III-4.) I have never seen this article.
[4] It should be noted in passing that Kaufmann refers only to Albright's general
remarks in *Archaeology and the Religion of Israel* (London, Oxford University Press,
1954), 121–125. Apparently he did not know of the monograph on the subject: 'The
List of Levitic Cities' (*Louis Ginzberg Jubilee Volume*, New York, American Academy
for Jewish Research, 1945, 49–73). But since Albright's position remains essentially
unchanged, it is perhaps a point of no importance.

need for this task had ended: the service of a single Tent could not support the whole tribe. There was need, therefore, to break the link that bound it to the service of the Tent, and at the same time to provide for its sustenance. So *P*, while maintaining the rights of Levi to sacrificial gifts, develops a programme for giving its members cities and fields for cattle raising as well. But it was a utopian programme and remained utopian.

3. Kaufmann then pursues (*BAC*, 46–64) what was to me an entirely novel line of argument. He professes to find through the Pentateuch, Joshua and Judges, 'an unreal utopian conception of the Land of Israel' (*BAC*, 46) which has boundaries at once much wider and much narrower than the actual holdings of Israel, and which corresponds thus neither to the actual areas occupied by the Israelite tribes nor to the Empire of David and Solomon (*BAC*, 48). In fact, there are in the Bible *five* distinct 'maps' of the Land of Israel, which correspond to changes in the historical situation, the first four of which are *ethnographic,* the last *imperialistic.*

The first is the 'Land of Canaan' as that had been promised to the patriarchs (*BAC*, 48–51). This picture of the land dominates the Pentateuch, especially from Gen. 12 to the end of Numbers. Its dimensions are huge: from Egypt (or the desert) on the south, to the Euphrates on the north (e.g. Gen. 15.18; Ex. 23.31; Deut. 1.7; Josh. 1.4). But it notably did *not* include Transjordan. The patriarchs roam in western Palestine, but only pass through Transjordan; the spies (Num. 13.21 ff) explore only western Palestine; in fact, land east of Jordan is considered unclean (Josh. 22.19), and the desire of Reuben and Gad to settle there (Num. 32) is regarded as rebellion; the boundary list of Num. 34.1–12 (cf. vv. 10 ff) explicitly excludes Transjordan—as does the picture in Ezek. 47.15–20. Many inhabitants of the land are mentioned: Hittites, Hivites, Girgashites, etc., but notably not the Philistines (although the *ancient* Philistines, the Caphtorim, appear in the patriarchal narratives). The promise associated with the land is purely ethnic: Israel is to occupy it all, expel or extirpate the inhabitants, and divide it all. The Pentateuch (e.g. Num. 34) does not know of a partial occupation or a partial division of the land.

Next comes what Kaufmann calls 'Moses' Land of Israel' (*BAC*, 51 f). This 'map' appears first in Num. 21.21–35, and reflects a discrepancy between the older ideal picture and the actual situation that emerged. It arose out of the fact that Israel conquered, and then occupied, a good part of Transjordan, although they had not intended to do so, but rather to pass through peacefully, and although it had not been promised to the patriarchs. So the land east of Jordan was added to the 'map' of Israel, the other limits of which remained as ambitious and as utopian as ever.

Next comes 'Joshua's Land of Israel' (*BAC*, 52 f). This 'map' prevails from Josh. 1 to Judg. 3, and was drawn by the wars of conquest. The old 'Land of Canaan' had been thought of as a single territorial unit, to be occupied and divided in its entirety. Not so Joshua's land. It included in Transjordan land never promised, but actually occupied and divided, while west of the Jordan it included: land both conquered and allotted, land allotted but never conquered (i.e. the coast plain, the Emek, foreign enclaves here and there), and land—of the older ideal picture— neither conquered nor allotted (from Lebanon northward). As Kaufmann points out (*BAC*, 79), the Joshua stories notably do not mention the Philistines, and so must have arisen before the Philistines of the Pentapolis arrived. The 'map' of Joshua was also drawn before the northern migration of Dan. Joshua's land was thus a mixture of actual and utopian features. And Joshua left as his legacy to Israel (cf. *BAC*, 57) the completion of the conquest (Josh. 13.1–6; 23.1–13; cf. Judg. 2.1–5; 20–3.4). The fact that all these passages are of the Deuteronomic frame of the book does not trouble Kaufmann, as we shall see.

This leaves two more 'maps', one ethnic and one imperialistic, but neither utopian: the 'Real Land of Israel' and the 'Empire' (*BAC*, 53 f). The first is the actual area of Israelite settlement, extending 'from Dan to Beersheba' (the expression first occurs in Judg. 20.1), of course with foreign enclaves here and there. The impulse to complete the conquest petered out, in good part because the clans had no further need or desire to expand. The last 'map', that of the 'Empire', is of course self-explanatory: it corresponds to the actual dimensions of David's state, which included the area occupied by Israel and a considerable foreign territory besides.

From all this, Kaufmann comes to a novel conclusion: each of these maps reflects a stage in Israel's history, and each is balanced by a corresponding stratum in the ancient biblical literature (*BAC*, 62). The impetus to conquer the land arose from the ancient promise to the patriarchs. This dream first collided with reality in the conquest of Transjordan, while Joshua's exploits gave it a partial—but only a partial—fulfilment. 'Joshua's Land' itself included utopian aspirations: to finish the job. But all hope of this soon flickered and died and, indeed, was already a dead issue by the period of the Judges. After Judg. 2–3 no more is heard of it (*BAC* 57–62). From this Kaufmann (*BAC*, 63 f) draws a conclusion that will require careful examination: since the pragmatic framework of Judg. 2–3 is concerned with a problem wholly without relevance in the seventh century, and long a dead issue, it follows that the view that this framework is a product of the seventh century Deuteronomists cannot be correct. True, the style is Deuteronomic, but this is an ancient style. The book of Judges, stressing as it does the chaos and corruption of the period, is in a real sense an idealization of the monarchy, and was written in the glorious days of David and Solomon. Joshua, as we shall see, is earlier still.

4. Kaufmann turns at length (*BAC*, 64 ff) to an analysis of the conquest stories themselves. Here, it must be said, there are many fine insights, and much that is in healthy contrast to the nihilism of Alt and Noth, with whom Kaufmann especially takes issue.

His remarks on the aetiological factor (*BAC*, 64 f, 70–74), in particular, might well cause one to applaud and underscore. That an aetiological element is frequently present he does not wish to deny. But can these stories be cavalierly dismissed as 'aetiological legends'? Here Kaufmann makes what is to me an exceedingly sound point (*BAC*, 71): 'Only those legends can be considered truly aetiological which *owe their existence* to the aetiological motive'. Can it be proved that any of the stories of Joshua fall in this class? On the contrary, the phenomena supposedly so explained are uniformly so commonplace: a pile of stones, a cave, some trees —that it is hard to see why anyone would want to 'explain' them. There is a cairn in the Vale of Achor—and the Achan story; another cairn at Ai—and a different story. There was also a cairn of stones over Absalom's grave (II Sam. 18.17 f), and a pillar erected in his memory which bore his name 'unto this day'. Is the Absalom story, then an 'aetiological legend'? Not at all! Such things as these may be drawn into a legend secondarily, but the legend did not come into being through them.

Or, take for example that story of Makkedah (*BAC*, 72 f): the five kings blocked in the cave and then hanged on five trees (Josh. 10.16–27). Did a cave blocked with stones and five trees really create this story?[1] Caves are in dozens of Bible stories—

---

[1] So maintained in the Alt school: cf. especially M. Noth 'Die fünf Könige in der Hole von Makkeda', *PJB*, 33 (1937), 22-36; K. Elliger, 'Josua in Judäa', ibid, 30 (1934), 47-71.

from Saul having his skirt cut off in one, to Obadiah hiding the prophets of Yahweh from the wrath of Jezebel in one—for, after all, caves are everywhere in Palestine. Are all these stories like-wise aetiological? As for trees, they too are everywhere. Why should the ones at Makkedah (and, be it noted, the Bible does not say that there were just five trees there, but that five were used for hanging: the conclusion that there were just five is the critic's own), and they alone, produce a tale of hanging? Clearly trivial objects like these cannot *produce* legends, though legends may adhere to them. But the legend was there first; the aetiology was attracted to it secondarily. Surely Kaufmann has injected a dose of earthy common sense into the discussion!

With equal vehemence Kaufmann attacks the premise of Alt and Noth that the conquest narratives of Josh. 1–11 were origin-ally of only local or tribal reference. The premise, he says (*BAC*, 65) is 'simply postulated by dogma'. He points out that in the stories of Judges, contrary to those of Joshua, the local and tribal reference stands out. But this does not justify the conclusion that these were not of national reference from the beginning. As he justly observes (*BAC*, 66): 'History knows of many local events which became the occasion for national events, and of many local heroes who became national heroes'. The Song of Deborah, for example, is certainly cast on a national scale. It describes a war which is Yahweh's war: the tribes of Israel are expected to come to the aid of Yahweh and are cursed if they fail to do so. A national unity, Israel as a supra-tribal subject of action, is presupposed. It is therefore absurd to suppose that the prose stories of the Judges lacked this national reference, even though it is seldom or never stressed.

It is equally wrong, says Kaufmann (*BAC*, 67–69) to reduce the Joshua stories to a purely tribal reference. Even if the Benjamite provenance of Josh. 1–9 could be established, that would not prove these stories to be of purely local significance. After all, Benjamite bards might be assumed to have been as nationally con-scious as those of Issachar, Naphtali or Zebulun. But Benjamite origin cannot be proved. True, the action of Chs. 5–9 takes place in the corridor between the later holdings of Judah and Ephraim, which was to be the territory of Benjamin. But all wars are fought somewhere, and the land of Benjamin was the logical place to fight this one. As a matter of fact, Benjamin is not once mentioned in the stories, not even in connexion with the affair of Gibeon. The

only tribe to be mentioned by name is Judah, and that in connexion with the story of Achan. To pin the stories to Benjamin by
localizing them at the shrine of Gilgal is a subjective phantasy:
there is no allusion to that shrine in Joshua (the circumcision was
not performed at the shrine, and was only done in Gilgal because
the Israelite camp was there). Kaufmann concludes (*BAC*, 70) by
asking why, if the stories of both Joshua and Judges were originally of local significance only secondarily subjected to a national
redaction, the tribal element has been so completely expunged
from Joshua alone, and not from Judges. The answer, he says, is
that no 'national redaction' ever had need to expunge the tribal
element. The national character of Josh. 1–11 is original, and the
fact that Judges has less of this but reflects the historical reality of
a certain weakening of national unity in the latter period.

5. Skipping further details, we press on to Kaufmann's reconstruction of the actual history of the conquest (*BAC*, 91–97).
Although he begins by admitting that the actual events are
'shrouded in a mist of legend', he believes it possible to recover the
essentials of what happened. It must be said that this turns out to
be an almost literal reconstruction of the narrative as told in
Joshua.

The Canaanite population lacked unity, but they were better
armed than Israel and could be overcome only by a unified effort.
The unity of the Israelite clans was based on the covenant made in
the wilderness and was symbolized by the prophetic leader who
stood at the head of the people. Now the greatest threat to
Israelite unity at the time (*BAC*, 92) was land-hunger: that individual clans would simply settle (as Reuben and Gad wanted to
do) and let the others get along as best they could. It was Joshua's
genius that he was able to separate conquest from occupation: he
kept the people in camp. Through all the war not a single city was
occupied. Indeed, that is why such places as Jericho and Ai were
put under ban.

But Joshua was also concerned to keep up the morale of the
people. This is why he never missed the opportunity to have an
impressive ceremony: the stone heap at Gilgal, the circumcision,
the altar on Ebal, and the like, are examples. Joshua's strategy was
sound. Not only was his plan of campaign brilliant and successful,
he maintained his base camp in Gilgal because, having ruined the
agriculture of Canaan, he had to get supplies from over the Jordan
(*BAC*, 95). With his rich booty of silver and gold, he was no

doubt even able to purchase supplies from Moab and Ammon too. The details of the campaign are seen, as we read, to be precisely those of the book of Joshua. Judg. 1 (*BAC*, 86) is the continuation of Joshua, and describes the wars of the tribes after the major conquest was complete. It was composed early in the period of the Judges (*BAC*, 84).

As for the composition of Joshua (*BAC*, 97 f), Kaufmann concludes that it too was composed at the very beginning of the period of the Judges, and by an author who 'wrote in an ancient Deuteronomistic style'. He had at his disposal such sources as the Book of Yashar, the border and city lists (which then included town lists for Ephraim and Manasseh), plus a priestly scroll concerning the conquest and division of the land, which contained a list of Levitical cities. Ch. 23 was the original conclusion of the book, together with 24.28–33 (24.1–27 was added later). The book was subjected, finally, to a 'still later Judahite edition' (one supposes Kaufmann puts this in the seventh century), in the course of which the city lists of Ephraim and Manasseh were removed.

2

But what evaluation shall we make of this work? In particular, has it provided an effective answer and antidote to the methods of the Alt-Noth school? I must say that, while I once more apologize for venturing criticisms upon so limited a basis, I do not think so.[1]

To be sure, many things are to be said in praise of Kaufmann. His criticisms of Alt and Noth, even though one may not agree with every detail of his argument, are often trenchant, well deserved and telling. Especially is this true of his rebuke of the absurd overplay of the aetiological factor, to which we have already alluded, as well as of the doctrinaire insistence that the Joshua stories must be of purely local significance. In his refusal of a Josianic date for the city lists in Joshua, I should, for one, agree. His evaluation of the conquest narrative is, if not altogether convincing, at least a healthy corrective and a refreshing contrast to overmuch nihilism. Beside all this, the reader will be certain to

---

[1] After the MS of this study had gone to the publisher, I received a copy of a most penetrating evaluation of Kaufmann's work by O. Eissfeldt: 'Die Eroberung Palästinas durch Altisrael' (*Die Welt des Orients*, 1955, 158–171). I am deeply grateful to the author for making this available to me, and I only regret that it reached me too late for it to be taken into consideration in this study. I feel, however, that Prof. Eissfeldt's conclusions are in essential agreement with my own, although the arguments presented in his paper and here are by no means identical.

note a host of detailed observations, far more than it has been possible to indicate here, that will appear to him penetrating in the
extreme. The very least that one can say of Kaufmann's book is
that it is stimulating. It is stimulating because the author is possessed of a keen, argumentative mind, is fully conversant with the
material, and approaches it from an entirely novel point of view:
a combination that is bound to produce fresh insights. For my
own part, I must confess that I have read few books recently in
which I have marked up the margins more disgracefully—and that
is always an indication of wakefulness! Even if one cannot always
agree, one is forced continually to rethink.

Nevertheless, there are many points that arouse question and
demand to be considered.

1. To begin with, even before one has read far enough to have
grasped Kaufmann's conclusions, or to be in a position to evaluate
them, one has thrust upon him certain features in the presentation
of the argument that tend to damage confidence in the out-
come.

For one thing, there is in it a good deal of the *non sequitur* and not
a little begging of the question. An example or two must suffice;
we shall return to the subject below. Thus one reads (*BAC*, 4)
that the seventh-century edition of Deuteronomy added only the
legislation regarding the unification of the cult, all the rest of that
book being older (a begged question unless the author has established the point elsewhere; but he makes no references). Then,
observing that the framework of the book of Deuteronomy (Chs.
1–11; 27–34) makes no mention of centralization, he goes on to
say: 'Hence the whole historical philosophy of Deut has no
original connection with the idea of the unification of the cult and
is older than it' (a *non sequitur* unless the question previously
begged be granted: *A* has no connexion with *B*, therefore *A* is
older than *B*). Then, having asserted (*BAC*, 4 f) that the first allusion to the idea of unification to be found in the Former Prophets
(save a gloss in Josh. 9.27) is in I Kings 3.2, he goes on to beg the
question by declaring that the material before that point, while
akin in style and idea to *D*, has contact only with the 'early' *D*. He
makes this statement without saying how one tells the style of
early *D* from that of late *D*; indeed (p. 7), he implies that one cannot. He then further commits *non sequitur* by arguing that, since
there is no mention of unification in Joshua and Judges, 'It follows
that the Deuteronomistic element in Josh and Ju is early and

has no connection with the seventh century' (*BAC*, 6). But it does not follow! In I Kings 3.2 the historian as good as explains why the subject has not been brought up before: the temple had not been built! The fact that Joshua and Judges do not mention unification proves no more than that they do not mention Solomon—or Josiah for that matter. Suppose a history of the U.S.A. does not mention the problem of secession in the chapters on the War of Independence. Does that prove that those chapters were written before Abraham Lincoln's day? Does, then, the absence of mention of unification in Joshua prove anything at all about the date of its composition?

Again, having pointed out that the problem of the incompleted conquest, so central in Joshua and Judg. 2–3, drops entirely from view after that point (save for Ps. 106.34), Kaufmann goes on to say (*BAC*, 62 f) that it is thus clear that that problem had its 'life-root in the events *of the period of the Conquest*'. That is a *non sequitur*, for all that has been proved is that the problem is rooted in the theology of the Deuteronomic framework of Joshua and Judges; it is also a begged question in assuming that this framework actually dates from the period of the conquest. But he then proceeds to a further *non sequitur* (*BAC*, 63): 'It follows, then, that the pragmatic framework of Ju is concerned in Ju. 2–3 with a special problem which was unknown to later generations. The view that this framework is "Deuteronomistic", a product of the 7th century or later, cannot be correct. In the 7th century there was no question of completing the conquest.' Surely a *non sequitur* if ever there was one! Of course the completing of the conquest was no live issue in the seventh century! But it could very well be a live issue in the theology of history of a seventh-century writer. The evils of Reconstruction are no longer a live issue in the southern U.S.A., but they might be very much alive in a history describing the decades following the war between the States. Does the fact that the historian raises issues long dead in our day force us to date him, say, in 1870 when Reconstruction was a live issue? Are we, then, forced to date the composition of Joshua and Judg. 2–3 to a period when completing the conquest was a live issue? These are but random examples. Nor are they trivial faults in logic. As we shall see below, they vitally affect the validity of Kaufmann's conclusions.

Furthermore, Kaufmann at times seems to misunderstand the position of his opponents in debate, with the result that his arguments appear beside the point. For example (*BAC*, 41–46), in discussing the list of Levitical cities in Josh. 21, he sketches the positions of Klein (that the list represents actual Levitical settlements in the time of David) and of Albright (that it represents an ideal programme of approximately the same period), and proceeds to refute them by three lines of argument.[1] He seeks to prove that the list is entirely Utopian in character and arose in priestly circles at the time of the conquest. This is not the place to enter into a detailed discussion of Kaufmann's arguments, although I feel that all of them are open to question.[2] But it is the second of these arguments, and seemingly the most telling, that betrays a fundamental misunderstanding of the issue. Kaufmann reasons that the artificial segregation of priests and Levites by families that the chapter exhibits, with all priests placed in the southern part of the land and all Levites in the north, makes clear the Utopian character of the list and forbids us to relate it to any actual situation—specifically not to the age of David. It is a priestly idealization from the days of the conquest. Now the chapter is undoubtedly an idealization, and one that certainly does not fit as it stands in the age of David. But, then, no one has said that it does. Albright, at least,[3] has argued only that the *bare list* of towns dates to the period between Saul and Solomon; he did not argue that the chapter as a whole (which is *P*) does so. And the bare list makes no such segregation at all. Thus Kaufmann's most telling argument is seen to be beside the mark, betraying a lack of grasp of Albright's position,[4] as well as of the methods of form criticism by which Albright—like Alt and Noth—has operated. It must be said, too, that no effort is made to meet the archaeological evidence marshalled by Albright: that some of the towns mentioned did not exist until after the conquest period to which Kaufmann assigns the chapter.

[1] Cf. p. 61, and n. [3] and [4] for a sketch of these arguments and references to Klein and Albright.

[2] As for the first (if the list is of David's day, why are such well-known priestly centres as Shiloh, Nob, Bethel, Gilgal, etc., to say nothing of Jerusalem, omitted?), this has already in part been cared for by Albright ('The List of Levitic Cities', [op. cit. in n. [4] p. 61], 59 n. [24]). If the list has any historical basis at all, it would be the aim to settle Levites precisely *away from* such places. Besides, by David's day, Shiloh had certainly—and Nob had possibly—been destroyed.

[3] I regret that I have never had access to Klein's article, and so do not know what he said on the point.

[4] Perhaps this is partly explained by the fact that Kaufmann did not know of Albright's longer monograph, 'The List of Levitic Cities', op. cit in n.[4] p. 61. The point may not be fully clear in the briefer discussion in *Archaeology and the Religion of Israel*, op. cit. in n.[4] p. 61, 121–125.

The feeling, likewise, will not down that Kaufmann has on occasion failed fully to meet the position of Alt and Noth as well. To be sure, his criticisms of that position are often telling in the extreme, particularly where a one-sided overstress of the aetiological factor is concerned. But there are other places where his arguments seem scarcely apropos. For example (*BAC*, 67 f), he counters the Alt-Noth view that the stories of Josh. 1–9 are Benjamite tales passed down at the shrine of Gilgal, in part with the observation that neither Benjamin nor the *shrine* of Gilgal is mentioned in these chapters. But it is difficult to see what force this argument, even if correct, would have against the position of Alt and Noth. For these scholars would explain the absence of mention of Benjamin on the hypothesis that the Benjamite tradition has now become the normative tradition of 'all Israel': a specifically Benjamite reference is, therefore, no longer to be expected in these stories. As for the shrine of Gilgal, they simply argue that these traditions were perpetuated there. Since Gilgal—whether the shrine itself or not—is mentioned repeatedly in these chapters, I fail to see where Kaufmann's argument is a telling one. Kaufmann may well be more correct than Alt and Noth on this point, but this phase of his argument is certain to slide by their position and leave it undisturbed. It must also be said that Kaufmann's characterization of Noth's position (*BAC*, 10 f, cf. 15) is somewhat in the nature of a caricature. And caricatures seldom accomplish anything constructive in scholarly debate.[1]

One senses things of this sort as one reads. A certain mistrust of Kaufmann's conclusions is thereby created in advance. One feels that he is an advocate intent on making his case and that the evidence, if presented ably, is not presented wholly dispassionately. One is driven to wonder if his conclusions will not be too systematically consistent, and if evidence that might seem to weigh against them will be given full play.

2. With these questions in mind let us evaluate Kaufmann's results. First of all, we might ask if his reconstruction of the conquest events (*BAC*, 91–97) is fully satisfying. Does it consider all the evidence and meet all the problems in a satisfactory way?

---

[1] Equally to be regretted are such passages as those found in *BAC*, 8, where the critics have attributed to them 'the subjective aim of blurring over the archaic and utopian character of Josh'; or, ibid, 62, where it is said that criticism 'has sought by all the means in its power to obscure' the evidence. Is this really fair? However wrong-headed one may think one's opponents are, is one to allege that they have wilfully tried to obscure evidence? This is a serious charge. One ought to be prepared to back it up with tangible proof of intellectual dishonesty—or withdraw it!

Frankly, it does not. It is much too neat a picture to be convincing. Kaufmann concedes at the outset that 'the events of the conquest are shrouded in a mist of legend' (*BAC*, 91), yet he feels that it is possible through the mist 'to distinguish the actual march of events'. Very good! But when he proceeds to do this, he presents us with what turns out to be a virtual 'ditto' of the Joshua narrative accepted at face value. If he senses any problem in this narrative, he does not let us see what it is. It is hard, therefore, to see wherein he finds legendary material in it at all, or why he thinks it necessary to make such a concession. Indeed, since he holds (*BAC*, 97 f) that the book of Joshua was composed—with the aid of written sources at that—at the beginning of the period of the Judges, thus in living memory of the conquest events, it is difficult to see where any room is left for 'legend' at all. And, in practice, he leaves none.

To be sure, the conquest as Kaufmann paints it yields a very intelligent picture: its strategy is sensible, its tactics sound. Whether it will convince the sceptical is another question. Indeed, even those of us who allow far more historicity to the Joshua narratives than do Alt and Noth might well question if the mere fact that so consistent and harmonious a picture can be drawn from those narratives is proof that events happened just so. It might be held to prove no more than that the Deuteronomic historian, while working with ancient material with which he did not tamper in any essential way, was a good historian who knew how to paint his characters vividly, and who had, furthermore, a feeling for terrain and a sound tactical sense. In short, the picture of Joshua the able commander-in-chief and morale builder, with which we are presented, is *too* consistent. One fears that it has been achieved by overmuch modernization—and not a little imagination. For example, that base camp in Gilgal (*BAC*, 95) protecting supply lines reaching back into Transjordan, to Moab and Ammon, is surely a modernization! What do nomad clans know of Quartermaster services and logistics? Has he not confused Joshua's army with a modern one, or at least a Roman or Babylonian one? The excessive nihilism of Noth is not to be counteracted by an uncritical use of the traditions of this sort.

And, it must be said, so consistent a picture of the conquest is achieved only by ignoring a good deal of the evidence. The reader would never guess the complexity of the problem. The conquest is presented, precisely as the book of Joshua presents it, as a unified onslaught by all Israel under a single commander-in-chief. Even those of us who by no means discount the historicity of such a concerted attack as portrayed in Joshua may well regret this over-simplification. There is no adequate discussion of evidence from the Bible itself, as well as from other sources, that makes it clear that Israel's settlement was also a long and devious process. Indeed, one is distressed to note that Kaufmann's book makes little or no reference to archaeological evidence at all. Unless I missed something, the book contains *only one* reference to archaeology, and that in a footnote (*BAC* 77, n. 64) having to do with the problem of Ai.

Let us look at the reconstruction of the battle of Ai (*BAC*, 96). The participation of the men both of Bethel and Ai (Josh. 8.17) is taken at face value and used (n. 73) to elucidate the tactics employed. But there is no mention of the witness of archaeology that Bethel and Ai do not seem to have been occupied concurrently. It is assumed that Ai is a fortified town, as in the narrative, but there is no discussion of the archaeological problem thus raised, or of the various efforts to solve it. This is not, in fairness be it said, that Kaufmann is ignorant of the problem. In the footnote mentioned above he clears himself by declaring that conclusions drawn from the excavations at et-Tell have been over hasty: the whole mound has not been dug, and possibly further excavation would show it to have been occupied at the time. Then, with a shift of ground, he argues that Ai is at another place—though where he does not say. Then, with a still further shift of ground, he declares that Ai does not mean 'Ruin', but a heap of stones—a distinction which, even if correct, I must say is too nice for me. But, with the exception of this one instance, archaeology is not called upon at all.

3. Equally serious, however, from a methodological point of view is the fact that there lies at the basis of Kaufmann's work a literary criticism which is, to say the least, eccentric. While, as we have noted, he expressly disavows the abandonment of literary criticism, he certainly does not use it in any conventional way. It must be said, too, that he shows little awareness—certainly no application—of the methods of form criticism, and of their importance in tracing the history of the traditions before they found their present form in the Hexateuch documents.

As we have seen, Kaufmann holds that there is no 'Deuteronomistic historical work' (in the singular). Although the Former

Prophets received redaction in the seventh century, only Kings is a product of that period. Samuel exhibits no Deuteronomic traits at all. Joshua and Judges do, of course, but their kinship is to the 'early Deut' and they represent different stadia of it at that, Joshua having been written at the beginning of the period of the Judges, Judges at the beginning of the monarchy. As far as *P* is concerned, he holds it (*BAC*, 3 f) to be older than *D*, with some of its material (e.g. Josh. 21, which dates to the conquest period) very ancient indeed.[1] Thus the unity of both *D* and *P* is broken up, both representing styles which were written in Israel from earliest times onward (*BAC*, 7). The fact that a passage is in the style of either says, therefore, nothing about the date of its composition.

(*a*) Now it seems to me that this represents not only an abandonment of the accepted results of criticism, but an abandonment of sound critical method as well. For to distinguish between an 'early Deut' and a 'late Deut' in the manner that Kaufmann does, and to assert that such a style might have been written at any period, means no less than to discard style as an effective tool of the critical method.

Now it is, of course, a commonplace that the laws of Deuteronomy have a long pre-history and are, in many cases, of very ancient origin. No one would deny that today. It is generally conceded, too, that the narratives and other materials of Joshua and Judges (as is the case with each of the Pentateuch documents) are in many cases very ancient, having been taken over by the historian with a minimum of alteration. In this sense one may speak of an 'early' and a 'late' *D*. But what evidence is there that the framework of the Deuteronomic literature, marked by a uniform theology of history and homogeneity of style, is to be distributed at will through all periods of Israel's history from the beginning to the exile? All objective evidence for dating this style points precisely to the seventh and sixth centuries. One thinks of the book of Kings, admitted by all hands—including Kaufmann—to have been composed in this period; the prose of Jeremiah—which could not possibly date *before* that time; plus the fact, admitted by Kaufmann, that all the books Deuteronomy–Kings received editing then. Ancient their material may have been, but their common

---

[1] Cf. Kaufmann, 'Probleme der israelitisch–jüdischen Religionsgeschichte', *ZAW*, 48 (1930), 22–43, especially 32–43 also *idem*, 'Der Kalender und das Alter des Priesterkodex' *Vetus Testamentum* IV (1954), 307–313.

style points to their definitive composition in the seventh and sixth centuries.

Kaufmann does not, of course, deny this unity of style, but he does not allow that it can be used as a tool of criticism. By asserting that a Deuteronomic style might have been written at any date, he is able to break up the unity of the Deuteronomic literature: Joshua at one point, Judges at another, Kings at a third. He seems to make little or no distinction between the framework of these books and the material they contain as far as style is concerned. For example (*BAC*, 97), the author of Joshua 'collected the stories from living tradition and wrote them down in his own style' (cf. *BAC*, 7). But this ignores the fact that it is not the *stories* of Joshua (or Judges or Kings), but the *framework* of the book that exhibits this characteristic Deuteronomic style. In other words, the author of Joshua did *not* write these stories down 'in his own style'; he took over stories of a style markedly different from his own and incorporated them in his work. Each of the books Deuteronomy–Kings contains material of diverse origin, date, viewpoint and style; the framework of the Deuteronomic corpus remains, in style and viewpoint, stubbornly a unit.

Kaufmann nevertheless does break up this admitted stylistic unit and relegate its parts to dates ranging all the way from conquest to exile. By what objective canon does he propose to do this? He tells us quite plainly (*BAC*, 7): on the basis of *internal evidence alone*. Thus style, long regarded as one of the basic canons of criticism, is frankly neutralized.

(*b*) But if the above has aroused misgivings, Kaufmann's use of internal evidence as the one canon for fixing date is certain to occasion yet further qualms.

We have already had occasion to tax Kaufmann with certain fallacies in the presentation of his argument. Since these fallacies concern precisely his use of internal evidence, it is necessary that we return to them. As we have seen, he posits (*BAC*, 4–7) that the seventh-century *D* added only the command to unify the cult; therefore portions of the Deuteronomic literature that do not exhibit this feature are to be dated earlier. Since it first appears at I Kings 3.2, only the book of Kings is to be placed in the seventh century. Again (*BAC*, 62 f), since concern for the completion of the conquest was a dead issue in the seventh century, and since this same concern is very much alive up to Judg. 3, it follows that Joshua was composed at an earlier period when the issue had actuality. Further (*BAC*, 46–62), having isolated five 'maps' of the 'Land of Israel', he concludes (*BAC*, 62) that each 'map' corresponds to a stratum of biblical literature which must come from the period that its 'map' reflects. Since Joshua's 'map' knew of nothing after the northward migration of Dan (Josh. 19.47)—and does not indeed know the details of Dan's northern holdings—its composition must be placed not long after that event (*BAC*, 7, 18, 44, 57, etc).

Now the above lines of argument are without exception *non sequitur*. Such use of internal evidence may at best help to determine the date at which certain of the material of the Deuteronomic books arose; it can in no case fix a *terminus ante quem* for the composition of any one of them. The fact that unification of the cult is not mentioned before I Kings 3.2, and the demand to finish the conquest not after Judg. 3, proves nothing whatever. That a history of the U.S.A. should tell of the land-hunger and westward expansion of the early settlers does not prove that the chapters that do so were written before that westward expansion ceased. Conversely, that there should be no mention of Robert E. Lee until the chapters dealing with the Civil War does not prove that the earlier chapters, where he does not appear, were written by an earlier author who had no knowledge of him. Yet this is just the sort of argument that Kaufmann tries to carry through.

As for the assertion that the various 'maps' must correspond to strata of literature composed in the periods the various 'maps' reflect, that is surely a resounding *non sequitur*. A history of Virginia, for example, could describe the 'map' of the royal land grant (west to the Mississippi, including Kentucky and a good part of the Middle West); the 'map' of the actual settlement a few decades later (scarcely west of Tidewater); its 'map' as one of the original thirteen states (gradually shrinking with the cession of land beyond the Ohio in 1784, and of Kentucky in 1792); its 'map' from 1792 until the Civil War (including what is now West Virginia); its post-bellum 'map' (with a strong, but gradually diminishing, feeling of Irredentism in the border counties of the new West Virginia); and so on down to the political and economic 'map' of the present-day state—and all in one book by one author. That various 'maps' of the 'Land of Israel' are to be seen in the Bible is certainly true. That there was a tension between the ideal and the actual dimensions of the land is likewise true. But to peg each 'map' to a corresponding stratum of biblical literature, and by this means to fix the date of these strata, is impossible. The fact that the 'map' of Joshua knew of nothing beyond the northward migration of Dan proves only that much of the material in Joshua is ancient—which few would deny; it proves nothing about the composition of the book itself.

Internal evidence can fix the date only of the immediate unit in which it is found; it can never fix the date of a book as a whole unless it has first been proved by other means (and here style must be called into the question) that that book is in fact in all its parts a unified composition. On the other hand, unless the unity of the Deuteronomic literature can be broken up by objective canons which prove that its framework could not, and in fact did not, come from a common period—specifically that of the seventh century—all the above argument is worthless. Of course one can prove by internal evidence that stories and lists in Joshua did not arise at a late date and conversely, of course, that those of Kings could not have arisen at an early date. But this does not break up the unity of the work itself, for this rests in its framework, not in the material it contains. We are left, then, with the stubborn fact that the framework of the Deuteronomic corpus is stylistically and theologically a unit; the effort to set it apart by internal evidence alone cannot be carried through.

4. It seems to me that, for reasons that I cannot grasp, Kaufmann is concerned to defend the unity of the canonical books. Deuteronomy, Joshua, Judges and Kings are separate books written by separate authors at different dates: this Kaufmann seeks to prove by internal evidence. As for Joshua, it seems to me that he has failed to grasp the distinction between: the date of the origin of much of the material (often very ancient); the date at which many of these traditions received final, fixed form, whether orally or in writing (hardly later than the days of David and Solomon); and the date at which the material was brought to its present form in the Deuteronomic corpus (seventh century). It is because of this fact—essentially a failure to understand the nature of current studies in the individual units of tradition within the literary documents—that he has been betrayed into a misuse of internal evidence. Internal evidence can fix the date only of the unit in which it is found—never of an entire book, unless it has first been proved by other means that that book is in fact a literary unit. It is because internal evidence shows much of the material in Joshua to be very old, and because the above distinction has not

been grasped, that Kaufmann is obliged to save the antiquity of the tradition by moving the composition of the entire book back to the very morrow of the events described. But this is a fallacy of method. The gap between the finished form of the tradition and the events cannot be bridged in this manner.

One must, therefore, reluctantly conclude that, in spite of his many merits, Kaufmann has not provided an adequate answer or a sufficient antidote to the methods of the Alt-Noth school. It is necessary, then, that we return to the latter subject once more.

CHAPTER FOUR

THE SCHOOL OF ALT AND NOTH

A Critical Evaluation

L ET us proceed, then, to an evaluation of the methods of the Alt-Noth school, particularly as these have been systematically developed and applied in the work of Noth. In doing so, it would be well if we were to avoid a piecemeal criticism, the endless debating of points of detail, and were rather to attempt to weigh the approach as a whole. We shall be concerned with the questions: is this approach methodologically sound? Does it produce satisfying results? And, if not, wherein lie its weaknesses? Particular points will be discussed only as they seem symptomatic of the underlying method.

I

If one begins—as one certainly should—by seeking for points of merit upon which to lay the finger, one has no difficulty at all. Indeed, so many are these, and so massive is the learning and so relentless the logic with which the whole structure is supported, that one is moved in the first instance to admiration.

1. The approach is sound, first of all, in that it takes its start from, and is firmly based in, the methods and assured results of literary criticism. This is both evident and expressly developed in the opening pages of Noth's great methodological work (*UG*, 1–44). The closely reasoned analysis of the sources offered there makes it clear that Noth begins his work with his feet firmly planted on the documentary criticism of the past. True, he has elsewhere[1] struck new paths in criticism, especially as regards the relationship of the Tetrateuch to the Deuteronomic corpus, the structure of the Deuteronomic corpus itself, and the problem of the documents in Joshua. But much of this seems very sound, and none of it represents a retreat from literary criticism as such. Alt and Noth are thus, in this respect, heirs of the classic Wellhausen tradition; they share with that tradition the merit that their approach to history begins with a critical scrutiny of the documents.

[1] Especially, *Überlieferungsgeschichtliche Studien I* (Halle, M. Niemeyer, 1943).

And it might be submitted at this point that all sound history writing must begin so. It ought to be a first principle that history writing cannot begin until the documents of history have been isolated, placed in their proper historical setting, examined for whatever bias or tendency they may have: in short, evaluated as sources of history. To be sure, the day has passed for such over-clever analysis as older scholars were often guilty of, the splitting of a verse between two or three sources and a couple of redactors —a *reductio ad absurdum* of critical method. Yet, if Noth on occasion exhibits more precision in this regard than one can follow, surely he is right in holding to the methods and assured results of literary criticism. Kaufmann, it must be said, is an illustration of what happens when this is not done.

2. Again, the Alt-Noth school is surely correct in its understanding that documentary criticism is only the beginning, that one must seek to press behind the documents into their pre-history. Here Alt and Noth have gone far beyond the Wellhausen school, which too often imagined that to date a document determined the age and value of its contents. This school knows well that such is not the case. On the contrary, even the latest documents contain material of the greatest antiquity. The historian, therefore, cannot stop with the finished document, but must ask after the origin of its material.

We must, therefore, make it quite plain at the outset that we have no quarrel with the term *Überlieferungsgeschichte* (Tradition-History) as such, nor with the task involved in tracing it. For, if we may put it so, the *Überlieferung* assuredly had a *Geschichte*! Between the original *Sitz im Leben* of the individual traditions, and the finished form of those traditions in the Pentateuch documents, there was certainly a long and complex history of transmission, oral or written, or both. Anything that can be done to elucidate that history is clear gain. It is only as the original *Sitz im Leben* of a tradition is understood that that tradition can be constructively evaluated. Whatever one may say of Noth's results, there can be no quarrel with the effort to trace the history of tradition as such. And, properly controlled, such results can be most constructive indeed.[1]

---

[1] The schools of Alt himself and of Albright have been especially fruitful in this regard, but a full bibliography would take pages. As examples of what we have in mind, cf. Alt, 'Das System der Stammesgrenzen im Buche Josua', (*Sellin-Festschrift* [Leipzig, A. Deichert, 1927], 13–24; reprinted in *KS* I, 193–202); Albright, 'The List of Levitic Cities', (*Louis Ginzberg Jubilee Volume* [New York, American Academy for Jewish Research, 1945], 49–73).

Nor have we a quarrel *per se* with the *method* by which Noth seeks to trace tradition history. Its first step is modest, not new, and indeed no more than an extension of literary criticism. We refer to the manner in which Noth (*UG*, 40–44), from a comparison of *J* and *E*, comes to the conclusion that *E* does not depend on *J*, nor *J* on *E*, but that both go back to a common *Grundlage* (*G*). *G* may be assumed to underlie wherever *J* and *E* run parallel, although the fragmentary state of *E* prevents the full reconstruction of it. If *J* is to be dated approximately in the tenth century, this would mean that G must be placed before the rise of the monarchy. Thus, by a deduction from documentary criticism, the horizons of the history of tradition are pushed a step farther back. This, however, is not new; others had already based themselves on a similar deduction.[1]

Noth, to be sure, is at times too hasty in his deductions regarding *G*. For example, (*UG*, 120–4), he reasons that the Hebron-Mamre traditions were no original part of the Abraham cycle because, lacking in *E*, they were not a part of *G*, but represent a later addition by *J*. But if, as Noth has agreed (*UG*, 42), *E* is too incomplete to allow a full reconstruction of *G*, this is to exceed the evidence. If *J* and *E* are parallel, we may affirm the presence of *G* behind them; but if they are not, it is risky to assume its absence.

But if we cannot be dogmatic about the extent of *G*, to establish the fact of it is clear gain. Noth is thus able to go behind von Rad's position and to trace all of the major themes of the Pentateuch, plus the 'all Israel' orientation of the tradition, back to *G*— hence to the period of the Judges. Thus an important step in the history of tradition is made.

Beyond this modest beginning, however, the Alt-Noth school seeks to attack the history of tradition by the methods of form criticism. And, once again, we must make it clear that we have no quarrel with those methods *as such*.

The methods of form criticism were first applied to Old Testament studies by H. Gunkel and his school. No one who is aware of the epoch-making importance of Gunkel's work can doubt the constructive value of the method, if properly controlled.[2] The methods of Gunkel have been further sharpened by Alt and Noth

---

[1] e.g. R. Kittel, *GVI*, I, 249 ff.
[2] Especially Gunkel-Begrich, *Einleitung in die Psalmen* (Göttingen, Vandenhoeck & Ruprecht, 1933).

and applied with *éclat*, particularly to the early traditions of Israel.
And the results have by no means been barren. One has only to
think of Alt's fundamental work on the law to realize that this
method, at its best, can be constructive in the extreme.[1] Let us,
then, make it quite clear that whatever quarrel we may have with
Noth, it does not revolve about the task of *Überlieferungsgeschichte*
or its method *per se*.

3. Finally, let it be said that the work of Noth is intrinsically
of such great importance that it cannot be brushed aside. Disagree
with it, perhaps; scoff at it, no! One is required to take it very
seriously.

By this it is not meant merely that one may learn a great deal
from Noth. Of course one may! His works exhibit tremendous
learning; they are, indeed, triumphs of a logical, orderly mind.
That there are insights of penetration and value in them to the
right and to the left is no more than one would expect of a scholar
of Noth's stature, trained in the school of Alt. But we do not refer
to points of detail, but rather to something of an all-over nature:
a caution, a corrective, if you will. Noth's whole treatment of
early Israel's traditions, much as one may disagree in general and
in detail, is at least a timely warning that certainly needs to be
heard against a too uncritical use of these traditions. His over-
scepticism is a warning against overmuch credulity, his remorse-
less method against slovenly method. One is enjoined against the
making of rash combinations, downright statements on the basis
of flimsy evidence, elaborate reconstructions of the events that are
supported by hypothesis only. One may—and for my part, I do—
recoil from Noth's nihilistic treatment of Moses and the Sinai
events, but one may not draw a more positive picture merely because one wishes it to be so. It must ever be remembered that
much about early Israel is, and will remain, unknown.

The traditions are, as Noth insists, the traditions of the Twelve-
Clan League. Nor may we doubt that they reached their normative
form after the settlement in Palestine. The historian must use them
with the full understanding that this is so. This means that, in
writing early Israel's history, he must never oversimplify. He has
continually to look behind the traditions, with their schematized

---

[1] Alt, *Die Ursprünge des Israelitischen Rechts* (Leipzig, S. Hirzel, 1934; reprinted in
KS I, 278–332). A recent, splendid example of form-critical method is G. E. Menden-
hall, 'Covenant Forms in Israelite Tradition', *BA* XVII-3 (1954), 50–76; cf. *idem*,
BA, XVII-2, 26–46. (Both reprinted as *Law and Covenant in Israel and the Ancient
Near East* [Pittsburgh, The Biblical Colloquium 1955].)

'all Israel' frame of reference, to events that were vastly more complex than the Bible narrative indicates. While it would be rash to deny (especially in view of the Ras Shamra texts) that long sagas, or epics, might have been developed even in the patriarchal age, it would be equally rash to insist that a connected epic of the Hebrew ancestors existed so early. Still less can the historian, on the basis of this material, engage to reconstruct the actual, chronological sequence of events. More than that, although he may not share Noth's nihilism *re* archaeological evidence, he would do well to remember that not one single event in the story of patriarchs, exodus and conquest can be proved from that quarter to have happened 'just so'.

In other words, all that we know of Israel before the settlement comes to us from the normative tradition of the later Twelve-Clan League. One need not discount the historicity of those traditions as Noth does, but one must realize that they are not historical documents like, for example, those in the book of Kings. The historian must remember the type of material he is dealing with, and be cautious. In reconstructing the origins of Israel and her faith a great deal must be left open. If this means that the historian must use the words 'perhaps', 'it is possible', 'it seems probable', more lavishly than he would like to do, there is no help for it.

2

So much, then, for the *plus*. What of the *minus*? Let us begin with the question: has Noth succeeded in presenting a satisfying picture of the origins and early history of Israel? The answer must be: no. On the contrary, his presentation leaves one distinctly dissatisfied. Is this really all that an objective historian can say?

1. As we have seen, Noth is able to derive from the Bible very little of a positive nature regarding the story of Israel's beginnings. The reason for this is that his method forbids him to find any appreciable nucleus of historical fact in the biblical traditions in the form in which they have come down to us.

To be sure, he agrees that the patriarchs were people who actually lived, and their religion an historical phenomenon. But although many of the Genesis traditions reflect historical circumstances, scarcely a single one of them can be said in any strict sense to be 'historical'. The actual migrations of the Hebrew ancestors cannot be elucidated from them. The ancestors did not come from Mesopotamia at all; the patriarchs themselves belong not in Canaan, but on the desert fringe. The exodus and Sinai traditions rest in history. But these events happened to different groups at different times and, in any case, nothing can be said of their details. Moses, too, is an historical figure in the sense that he lived—or rather 'died'—but he was not the great founder of Israel's faith. He had nothing to do either with exodus or Sinai; he arose out of a grave tradition at home in the steppes of Transjordan. The Israelite settlement in Palestine happened, yes, and in so far is historical. But it was a vastly different process from that portrayed in Joshua, the narratives of which are largely unhistorical.

It is thus clear that Noth's method, whatever else may be said of it, issues in a very negative evaluation of the traditions. This does not, of course, prove that it is wrong. But it does at least allow us this negative criticism: it leaves many questions unanswered. Most serious of these is, in my opinion, *that the origin of Israel and its faith is left quite without adequate explanation.*

(a) That the Israelite amphictyony with its Yahwistic faith was a going concern in the period of the Judges is, of course, beyond question. Now Noth says that neither the amphictyony nor its twelve clans existed prior to the settlement. What, then, possessed these clans, almost as soon as they came into being, to bond themselves together and adopt a common faith? In one sense, perhaps, one may justly decline to answer the question. Similar amphictyonies, as Noth has shown,[1] were widely instanced and no special explanation can be required of their origin. But that the question is a fair one, and demands an answer, is tacitly admitted by Noth himself, who asks (*GI*, 119): 'how it happened that, directly after the settlement, "Israel" felt itself to be so much of a unity that a structure of traditions arose which had as its subject a common pre-history of this "Israel".'

Why indeed? Noth goes on to say (ibid) that the question cannot be answered with any assurance 'since the tradition does not reckon with this happening and therefore says nothing about it'. True—yet not strictly accurate! The traditions *do* reckon with the origins of the Israelite covenant and faith, and Noth does not credit those traditions, namely: that the entity 'Israel' existed (albeit, we may agree, not in its later, normative form), and found its distinctive faith, *prior to the settlement*. Noth's explanation of the

[1] Noth, *Das System der zwölf Stämme Israels* (Stuttgart, W. Kohlhammer, 1930).

origin of 'Israel' and its faith is in any event a very lame one: that both developed gradually on the soil of Palestine, first as participants of the Sinai events introduced the worship of Yahweh, to be followed by others who had experienced the exodus and who gave witness to the mighty acts of the God who had delivered them. As the God of the exodus was identified with Yahweh of Sinai, and as the clans united in covenant league about this God, 'Israel' came into being (*GI*, 119 f).

Now none would deny that Israel's organization and faith underwent development in Palestine. But to posit a development is not to explain it. I should object that Noth has given no adequate explanation of why these scattered clans of diverse origin came together under a common faith in the first place—and did so so strongly that they at once began to posit that they had always had a common history—nor of the extreme suddenness with which, under his theory, this must have been done. It is scarcely 200 years from the final settlement of the clans in the thirteenth century, to the rise of the monarchy under Saul in the eleventh. Yet the 'all Israel' orientation of the traditions (it is common to *J* and *E* and therefore, in Noth's view, goes back to *G*) was already official before the end of that period. The amphictyony with its Yahwistic faith is clearly in operation by the time of Deborah (twelfth century). Could the various clans have settled, taken shape themselves, gradually developed and adopted a normative Yahwism, bonded themselves in covenant league around it, *and have developed a unanimous tradition that things had always been so* in so short a time? For my part, I find it incredible. It is far easier to believe in the existence of, and a connexion between, at least certain of the clans prior to the settlement, and the adoption by them of Yahwistic faith in the wilderness period.[1]

(b) Equally incredible is the explanation of Moses. How is his stature in normative Israelite tradition to be explained under Noth's view? The fact, which Noth and others have based themselves on, that the figure of Moses does not loom large in the early biblical traditions outside the Pentateuch is not really very impressive. Perhaps it no more than illustrates the fact that Israel's faith was not in Moses, but in Yahweh. How seldom, indeed, are any of Israel's heroes mentioned outside the literature that immediately

---

[1] Many of the older Wellhausen school who, like Noth, discounted the tradition of unified onslaught as found in Joshua, were driven by that very fact to find the beginnings of Israelite unity in the wilderness: e.g. A. Lods, op. cit., 309 f.

concerns them![1] On the other hand, the figure of Moses as leader of the exodus, founder of faith and lawgiver, is absolutely central in both *J* and *E* (and therefore in *G*), and thus may be assumed to have been so at least back to the period of the Judges. But if Moses was none of these things—if he was only some Transjordanian *sheikh* whose memory was enshrined in a grave tradition—how can it be explained that he so quickly came to be looked upon not only as the leader of all Israel, but positively as its founder?

Noth's explanation (*UG*, 190f) is peculiarly lame. The figure of Moses was drawn quite naturally from the grave tradition into the theme 'Entrance into the Promised Land', and thus into the tradition circle of central Palestine where Jacob was also at home. He thus became, save for Jacob, the oldest individual figure in the Pentateuch tradition, with the result that tales about him grew and grew. But to explain Moses so asks of me a degree of credulity that I cannot manage. The assumption that Israel's faith grew, as it were out of the ground, without founder, but then straightway felt so keenly the need for a founder that it was obliged to blow up the figure of the colourless Moses to gigantic proportions in order to accord him that status—is really past believing. No literal acceptance of rods turned to serpents or manna from heaven would require a more heroic *sacrificium intellecti* than this. It is far more soberly objective to look upon Moses—with full recognition of the problems entailed—as actually the lawgiver and founder. If to do so contravenes the thesis of the five separate tradition themes of the Pentateuch, it is to be regretted.

Now one could argue that it is unfair to ask the historian to explain everything. Some things we lack the knowledge to explain. Where this is so, the honest historian can only admit that he has no explanation. True! But it must be remembered that in this case the problem is in good part of Noth's own making. He has followed a method that reduces Israel's traditions—which *had* their explanation of origins—to a *nil*, and then is confronted by the *fact* of Israel, a fact for which he can provide no adequate explanation. Be that as it may, it certainly leaves us with the question if any history of Israel can be called satisfactory that leaves the major factor in that history, Israel's faith, so poorly accounted for. Granted that the traditions of early Israel were normalized in the

---

[1] For example, judging from the infrequency with which they are mentioned, one could similarly reason that neither Isaiah nor Jeremiah were known widely in Israel until the post-biblical period.

Twelve-Clan League, and thus have a national frame of reference which we may be sure was not original in all of them, does this force us to a complete mistrust of those traditions? May we not ask, at least, if the picture there given is not more credible in its broad outlines than the construction of Noth? May we not ask further if, when a method of criticism discards so completely the united witness of tradition and ends in a nihilism of its own making, it may not be the method itself that is at fault?

2. This brings us to a second observation of a negative sort regarding Noth's work. Not only is Noth unable to rely on the Hexateuch traditions for the writing of Israel's early history, *he is unable to fill the void thus created by an appeal to archaeological evidence*. Indeed, he exhibits a nihilism regarding archaeology that virtually denies it the right to speak to the point at all. And surely this is unsound.

We have had occasion to refer to this before.[1] The numerous parallels that archaeology has discovered between the Genesis narratives and second-millenium Mesopotamia neither impress Noth nor convince him that Israel's ancestors indeed migrated thence: all this is susceptible of other explanations. The heavy incidence of Egyptian names in the family of Moses and Aaron is no proof that these people were ever in Egypt: this too can be explained in another way. Again, archaeology proves that certain Palestinian towns, a number of them mentioned in Joshua and Judges as taken by Israel, were destroyed in the thirteenth century B.C. But this is no proof of the biblical tradition. After all, we have no reliable biblical tradition of these events in the first place—only aetiological tales. Indeed, there is not even any proof that the known destruction was made by Israel at all. It could, for all we know, be the work of the Philistines, or of some forgotten city king in some forgotten war.

Now before we counter that Noth is being wilful, let us grant the point: this is indeed not 'proof', if by 'proof' is meant irrefragable evidence that the Bible story happened 'just so'. The fact that the Laban-Jacob stories fit the *milieu* of second-millenium Mesopotamia does not prove one item of those stories to be true, but only that they were told by a people who were familiar with that, or a similar, environment. In spite of all the amazing evidence that archaeology has brought, not one single item in the entire Hexateuch tradition has been proved true in the strict sense of that

[1] Cf. pp. 54 f. and references there.

word. Archaeology cannot bring that sort of proof. We are warned, therefore, against downright affirmations of an 'archaeo-logy-proves-the-Bible' sort, such as are all too common in certain circles. But if dogmatic affirmation is not in order, neither is dog-matic denial!

The question is not: does archaeology 'prove' the biblical tra-dition? but: *where is the balance of probability in the matter?* That is, indeed, the area in which the historian usually labours. He weighs the evidence, *and does not brush aside the more probable for the less probable*.

This is not the place to marshal the archaeological evidence relating to the patriarchal narratives. Suffice it to say that it is massive. To mention but one thing, the nomenclature of Upper Mesopotamia as it is known from Mari and elsewhere certainly proves that a population akin to the Hebrews was to be found there in the patriarchal age. The Nuzi texts at least prove that the customary law of the patriarchs had its home in the same general area in approximately the same age. And much more. Put all this alongside the unanimous tradition of the Hebrews that their an-cestors migrated thence, and the objective historian ought to give in to the overwhelming balance of probability. As for evidence of the Israelite conquest, is archaeology really as helpless as Noth would have it? Can it not tell a Philistine occupation from an early Israelite one? Or a late Bronze Age Canaanite one from an early Iron Age one? Can it not tell if there has been an appreciable gap between destruction and re-occupation? Is archaeology, then, un-able to distinguish a destruction of the Amarna Age from one at the hands of the Philistines, and both from one occasioned by Israel (cf. *GI*, 70 f)? The fact is that archaeology shows that a row of towns, some mentioned in the Bible as taken by Israel, seem to have fallen to Israel in the thirteenth century. Admittedly this is not 'proof' of the Joshua narrative, but the probability of a con-nexion between the two is overwhelming.

What, after all, is 'proof'? If one were to see the print of a horse's hoof in the mud, one might rashly conclude that that is 'proof' that a horse had been there. Not so! However convincing it may be, it is no more than circumstantial evidence. It could have been the work of someone playing a prank! Proof, to stand up in court, must have eye witnesses: someone must have seen the horse. Now the evidence of archaeology, at least in the area with which we are concerned, is of necessity largely circumstantial; 'eye-witness proof'—in this case contemporary inscriptions—is seldom forthcoming. If the historian waits for it, as Noth seems to do (*GI*, 41f), he will wait long. But the historian does not work in the law court and cannot demand that kind of 'proof'. He is happy when he gets it, but most of the time he must be content with less direct evidence. And from that evidence he seeks the *balance of probability*. No history of Israel could ever be written—Noth's included—did the historian wait at every point for irrefragable 'proof' of the sort Noth demands.

I am convinced that at the bottom of Noth's scepticism *re* archaeology there lies precisely his method. Because of it, he tags the traditions 'aetiological tales' or whatnot, and so depreciates them that he can affirm that we have no reliable tradition of the capture, say, of Bethel or Lachish. At the same time, a wholly different theory of the conquest is advanced: first a peaceful search of seasonal pasture, then gradual settlement in open areas. Armed conflict, if such there was, represented only the last phase of occupation; but it was, in any event, rare (cf. *GI*, 58f). Then scepticism *vis-à-vis* tradition—itself the result of method—plus a preconceived hypothesis of how the settlement actually took place, 'gang up' on archaeology and deny it all relevance. *We have no archaeological evidence bearing upon the conquest narratives of Joshua because,* ex hypothesi, *there can be none.*[1]

3

We see, then, that Noth is driven by his method to a drastic devaluation of the biblical traditions. And this, plus certain preconceived theories regarding the actual course of events, leads him to an equal depreciation of the value of archaeological evidence. Since the real issue lies in the method itself, it is necessary that we proceed to a more detailed discussion of it.

W. F. Albright has already made a searching, if admittedly provisional, criticism of Noth on this score.[2] He points out that Alt and Noth stress three guiding principles in their studies in the field of Hebrew origins: a rigid application of the methods of form criticism; constant emphasis on the factor of aetiology in explaining the origin of tradition; emphasis upon the *Ortsgebundenheit*

---

[1] '*Einen sicheren Fall dieser Art aber haben wir bis jetzt noch nicht. Und das ist kein Zufall; denn ein solcher Fall ist auch gar nicht zu erwarten. Die israelitischen Stämme haben sich nicht durch gewaltsame Eroberung und Zerstörung kanaanäischer Städte Platz im Lande verschafft*—' (*GI*, 70).

[2] Albright, 'The Israelite Conquest of Canaan in the Light of Archaeology', *BASOR*, 74 (1939), 11–23. Reference to Albright in this section is to this article.

of tradition (i.e. the tenacity with which names and tales are supposed to adhere to geographical locations).

1. As for the first of these, there is little that can be added to what Albright has said. Albright freely recognizes the tremendously important contribution that form-critical studies have made, from Gunkel down to Alt himself. But he argues that there is a tendency in the Alt school to make form criticism carry more than its weight, even to the point of imagining that the historicity of a given tradition—or its lack of it—can be established by an examination of the literary form in which it is cast. Ancient bards and scribes had to conform, for lack of alternatives, to 'fixed patterns of oral delivery and formal styles of writing' (ibid, 12). Since this is so, form itself can never be the final arbiter of historicity: there must be external evidence. With this one can only agree.

Certainly form criticism is a necessary tool of the historian. Awareness of the form and type of a tradition will inevitably to some degree control its evaluation and interpretation. If the historian knows that he has to do with saga, he will not evaluate it as if it were the 'David Biography' or the annals of the kings of Judah. If he is dealing with epic material, he will treat it like epic. He will, for example, look out for formalized motifs, the subsuming of a whole group migration under the movements of the individual hero, and so on. Form criticism is indeed a control over exegesis and interpretation. But it cannot pass final verdict on historicity. The historian would do well to remember the sober words of Kittel (which I read after I had finished Noth and found like a breath of fresh air): 'A dilemma like the following: the patriarchal narrative is either history or saga, or as it might be put: the patriarchal narrative is not history but saga, is therefore entirely wrong. That narrative can be saga as well as history.'[1]

One might add that literary form does not, where the facts can be tested, furnish a final test of historicity. Certainly it does not do so today. A novel may be pure fiction or well-nigh autobiography; a newspaper dispatch may be a model of objective accuracy or the most vicious propaganda. Was it fundamentally otherwise in ancient times? The ancient had far fewer literary types to choose from than do we; he was, therefore, under even greater necessity of formalizing what he had to say. Is there any evidence that there were no degrees of historical veracity within a given form? On the contrary, we know that there was. Myths, for example, may con-

---

[1] R. Kittel, *GVI*, I, 270.

tain a greater or lesser degree of historical content.[1] The same is
true of epic poems. Some royal annals seem to be conscientiously
accurate; others are formalized boasting. By the same token, to
class a tradition as a cult legend says nothing *per se* regarding its
veracity: the legend might just possibly be correct! To be sure,
this is not to say anything very positive. But, since historical value
can be shown in certain known cases to vary within a given form,
it does warn us not to imagine that classification of form automatically renders verdict on historicity. Objective, external evidence
is always required.

2. Next, to the second guiding principle of the Alt-Noth
school: stress upon *aetiology as a creative factor in the formation of
tradition*. Here I wish again to second the arguments of Albright
and perhaps to reinforce them a bit. I am, indeed, prepared to go
quite far in this connexion, even to the point of 'jumping off the
deep end', for it seems to me that nothing is more fundamentally
wrong in the method of Alt and Noth than this. I should not wish
to deny that the aetiological factor is present and may have given
rise to many details in the tradition. But I should like to submit
that, *where historical tradition is concerned*, not only can it be proved
that the aetiological factor is often secondary in the formation of
these traditions, *it cannot be proved that it was ever primary*.

We have already noted the stress laid upon this factor by the Alt
school. Alt's own treatment of Joshua,[2] where practically everything in Josh. 1–9 is subsumed under this rubric is a classical example. But it is to be found everywhere. For example, the tale of
Jacob's purchase of land at Shechem (Gen. 33.19) grew out of the
fact that the later amphictyony owned land there (*UG*, 89f);
Jacob's pilgrimage from Shechem to Bethel (Gen. 35.1–5) is the
aetiology of a later cultic rite (*UG*, 87);[3] Abrahams's near sacrifice
of Isaac (Gen. 22.1–19) provides the aetiology of a local cultic
custom originally unconnected with Abraham (*UG*, 121 n. 317,

[1] Cf. F. M. T. deLiagre Böhl, 'Mythos und Geschichte in der altbabylonischen
Dichtung', (*Opera Minora* [Groningen, J. B. Wolters, 1953], 217–233). He compares
the figures of Gilgamesh, Adapa, Sargon of Akkad and Semiramis. All these figures
are cloaked in myth; but while the last two are clearly historical individuals, the first
two, Böhl thinks, probably are not. For my part, I should hesitate to declare even
Gilgamesh entirely unhistorical. But Böhl's point is certainly sound. Again, among
the Ras Shamra texts, the epics of Keret and Dan'el are much less purely myth-
ological than is the Baal epic, and may contain a kernel of legendary history (cf.
Albright, *Archaeology and the Religion of Israel*. [Baltimore, Johns Hopkins Press, 3rd
ed. 1953], 90.)
[2] Alt, *Josua*, (*BZAW*, 66 [1936] 13–29; reprinted in *KS*, I, 176–192).
[3] Cf. Alt, 'Die Wallfahrt von Sichem nach Bethel', reprinted in *KS*, I, 79–88.

126); the tradition of the double burial of Abraham and Sarah at Mamre (Gen. 23; 25.7–10) was suggested by the name of the cave Machpelah ('Double Cave': *UG*, 125); and so on.

The gravity of all this lies in the fact that, in the minds of Alt and Noth, when the aetiological factor is present in a tradition, that tradition is automatically suspect. It could hardly be historical, for the aetiological factor created it: an existing custom or land-mark is explained by telling a story about it. Aetiological tales arise to give answer to 'the eternal child's question, "Why?" '[1] I feel strongly that no single feature in the entire method of this school has been more productive of nihilism regarding the traditions than this.

The debate does not revolve about the presence of the aetiolo-gical factor (it is obviously and frequently present), but about the *priority of that factor in the formation of tradition.* Do tales with aetio-logical features *arise* out of the desire to answer the eternal *Kinder-frage* 'Why?' If it can be proved that such is the case, then the aetiological factor is primary and we must simply give in to Alt and Noth and accord such traditions little or no historical value. But if it can be proved that, at least sometimes, this is *not* the case —that sometimes the aetiological factor is purely secondary—then it is an extremely subjective procedure to discount the historical value of these traditions *short of objective proof.*

Now the aetiological factor is frequently the creative and de-terminative element in fable and fairy tale: why is the ocean salty? How did the camel get his hump? Where did the donkey get his loud, discordant bray? How did the crest of yon hill come to be cleft in twain? What giant's hand flung those islands far out to sea? Here is a *genre* of stories told precisely to answer the *Kinder-frage* 'Why?' But in such cases there is no question of historicity: the teller does not believe his own tale, and it is a question if the child to whom it is told believes it literally. As for myth, the case is less clear. Myth does deal with the origins of things, and so gives the answer to the question 'Why?' But these are scarcely 'child's questions'. And, although the myth was re-enacted in the ritual, it can hardly be said that the myth was concocted as an aetiology of the ritual. The myth of Marduk's conflict with the Chaos Monster was scarcely composed to explain what the Baby-lonians were already doing on New Year's Day—but quite the other way around. One might as well say that the narrative of the

---

[1] Alt, *Josua* (op. cit. in n. [2] p. 91), 182 f: '*Antworten auf die grosse Kinderfrage aller Zeiten "Warum?"* '.

Last Supper was invented to explain why Christians practice such a rite! If any do so say—well, it is going a bit too far!

Be that as it may, stories of aetiological flavour do exist in the Bible, which seem to have as their primary function the answering of the question 'Why?' One thinks of the story of the Tower of Babel, which explains the multiplicity of languages on earth, and which is made secondarily into an etymology of Babylon; or the story of the fall (Gen. 3), which explains why man must labour for his bread, why women suffer in childbirth—and why snakes crawl on the ground. But even in these cases it is more than a probability that the stories had had a long history before the aetiological feature was drawn in. One thinks, too, of certain stories that explain how certain heroes got their names: e.g. that of the birth of Jacob (Gen. 25.21–6), which is a play on the similarity in Hebrew of the words 'Jacob' and 'heel'; or that of the baby Moses (Ex. 2.1–10), where there is a pun on 'Moses' and the verb 'draw out' (*māšāh*). But, here again, it is probable that the aetiological factor is responsible only for a single detail of the story, and that we must reckon with the likelihood that the stories develop conventional motifs far older than the aetiology they are used to provide. In the case of Moses, if one remembers the stories of the birth and childhood of Sargon of Akkad, this would seem to be certain. The aetiology is, therefore, secondary.

In any event, our problem is not primarily with this *genre*, but with the factor of aetiology as it is to be observed throughout the traditions of the great Hebrew historical saga. The question is: can it be proved in the case of these national traditions that, where the aetiological factor is present, that factor is always—or even sometimes—primary and determinative in the formation of the tradition? We ought to recall in this connexion the sound observation of Kaufmann[1] that one ought not to speak of an 'aetiological tale' unless it can be shown that that tale *came into being* through the aetiological factor.

Now it seems to me that the assumption that such was actually the case can be tested *only in the full light of history*. We shall get nowhere if we confine ourselves to Israel's early traditions, for we do not in truth know how these traditions arose. We should only end up contradicting one another. Nor can we appeal to the traditions of other ancient peoples to settle the matter. In the first place, no other ancient people had traditions of origins comparable

[1] *BAC*, 71 etc; cf. p. 64.

to those of the Hebrews. In the second place, we are in no better position to control the origins of such traditions as exist. We can only, in the clear light of history, examine traditions that do have an aetiological element, *the origin of which we can trace*, in order to see if in such cases aetiology is necessarily, usually, or ever, the primary and controlling element. I stress this lest the examples shortly to be adduced should seem to some either frivolous or irrelevant.

That this is the correct procedure has been sensed by Albright, who brings forth a number of parallels from the traditions of the modern Arabs. That is, of course, the best place to look for parallels. The Arabs are a Semitic people who live in the land once occupied by Israel; and, furthermore, their traditions can to a degree be controlled. I regret that I am not competent to add further evidence from this quarter. But it would seem to me that, unless one is going to plead that its operation in ancient Israel was a special phenomenon, oral tradition might be expected to develop according to similar principles wherever it is to be found. In any event, an abundance of popular traditions can be found with a clear aetiological factor (i.e. the explanation of some known custom of landmark) where that factor is *demonstrably secondary*. This should at least warn us against a doctrinaire evaluation of the same factor in Israel's traditions.

In Plymouth, Mass., one may see on the beach a stone with a cupola erected over it; it will be pointed out as the very rock where the Pilgrim Fathers first stepped ashore. And 'there it is until this day!' Now it is not much of a rock, but it is at least as notable as that stone pile at Ai (Josh. 8.29), or that cave with five trees about it at Makkedah (Josh. 10.26f). It demonstrates in any case that there is an aetiological element in the tradition of the Pilgrims. If Alt's and Noth's application of the principle of aetiology be correct, we should be obliged to assume that the story of the Pilgrims, at least of their landing in Plymouth, is a tale concocted to answer the *Kinderfrage*: why is this notable rock here on our beach? But the facts are quite otherwise: the tradition was primary, the aetiology secondary. It is a question if the rock had anything to do with the landing of the Pilgrims. It seems to have been brought into the tradition about the time of American Independence; the structure that protects it dates only from 1920. The truth is that, if the story of the Pilgrims *had not already been normative*, no one would have given that rock a second thought.

Again: Americans have the peculiar custom on the last Thursday of November of celebrating Thanksgiving Day by going to church and then returning home to a bountiful turkey dinner. And many a child has asked his father, '*Warum?*' Corresponding to custom is, as one would expect, legend to explain it: our Pilgrim Fathers shot wild turkeys, harvested the pumpkins and the corn, and observed this custom in gratitude to God for his mercies—and we thus remember both God and them. A practitioner of tradition-history, however, can easily see that the custom created the legend; the legend, therefore, is unhistorical. Actually, of course, Thanksgiving is the survival of an ancient harvest festival the origin of which is unknown. But since it is observed both as a national and as a religious occasion, it is easy to see why the Pilgrims were drawn into it, for they are held to be the fathers of the nation (Virginia resents that! The legend has its *Haftpunkt* in Boston!) and men of exemplary faith. Such a religious-national custom would naturally be explained by telling a story about them. But, again, the facts are inconvenient. The story of the Pilgrim Thanksgiving, though no doubt dressed up in the telling, is historical (October 1621); the custom did not become normalized as a national holiday until the middle of the nineteenth century, though practised sporadically and locally before that time. Legend thus demonstrably precedes custom. Indeed, had not the legend existed it is doubtful if the custom would ever have arisen.

Again: the legend that George Washington once threw a dollar over the Rappahannock River at Fredericksburg, Va. The origin of this legend is obscure. It is enshrined in Parson Weems' edifying book,[1] but whether or not it originated in the fertile mind of the author I do not know. In any event it is very old; I had it first —from oral tradition—as a boy. Now any one who has followed the local newspapers (or those of Richmond or Washington, D.C.) in recent years might have read an account of how, in Fredericksburg as a part of the celebration of George Washington's birthday, there is an annual contest to see if any boy of the town can throw a dollar over the Rappahannock. Several, I understand, have succeeded, for the river is not over ninety yards wide just below the town at Ferry Farm, Washington's boyhood home, where the contest is held.

Here we have, then, a custom that requires explanation, and an

---

[1] The Rev. Mason L. Weems, *The Life and Memorable Actions of George Washington,* *ca.* 1800.

aetiological legend to supply it. Let us trace the history of that
tradition according to the principles of the Alt-Noth school.
George Washington was, of course, revered in the Thirteen-
Colony League, and in its successor the U.S.A., as the father of
his country. He is, thus, the sort of historical figure to whom
legends attach themselves. His birthday was early celebrated
throughout the Thirteen-State League as a national cultic festival
and, of course, nowhere more ardently than in Fredericksburg,
for here—tradition had it—was his boyhood home ('See, there is
the spot until this day!'). Now such occasions are usually observed
by means of sports, contests, and picnics with patriotic speeches in
which the normative traditions are frequently alluded to—and tend
to expand! So at Fredericksburg. In the course of such a picnic
long ago, we may imagine, one boy bet another a dollar that he
couldn't heave a rock over the river. And there it began. The
thing became a traditional event. Soon for the rock there was sub-
stituted a ball, and then for the ball a silver dollar; the boy who
could toss it to the opposite bank would win a prize. Then the
inevitable *Kinderfrage*: 'Papa, why do they do that every Washington's birthday?' And what answer could Papa give save that of
aetiology? 'Our father, George Washington, once did the same
thing at this very spot; we are celebrating his memory'. Then, as
pilgrims in great numbers began to come to Fredericksburg to
view the holy sites of the national founder, the legend was carried
by them to the farthest parts of the country. Thus we see how a
local aetiological legend takes its place in the normative tradition
of the Thirteen-State League!

The trouble about all this is that it is pure moonshine! Whether
the legend rests on fact or not I do not know. Washington was a
large and powerful man and could easily have done it—though
hardly at the age of eleven, as Parson Weems would have us believe. But that is not the point. The point is that, while an aetiological connexion between custom and legend is explicitly
affirmed, *the legend is demonstrably prior to the custom*. The custom, in
fact, began in 1936 for purposes, it is to be feared, of publicity—
and on the basis of the legend![1] Indeed, had it not been for the
legend no one would ever have thought of the custom. Of course,

---

[1] On the origin of the custom see 'Big Train vs. Big Myth', *Sports Illustrated*, Feb.
21, 1955, 61. 'Big Train', it should be explained, refers to Walter Johnson, one-time
star pitcher of the Washington 'Senators' and possessor of one of the most powerful
throwing arms in the history of baseball. He was brought down to initiate the custom
and, apparently, to make sure that the first test would succeed. It did!

in demonstrating its priority, the *historicity of the legend is neither affirmed nor denied.*

I am sure that Noth would object that these examples are irrelevant. The traditions of early America were developed in the full light of history, in an age of literacy, and are therefore in no sense parallel to the traditions of early Israel. I fear, too, that he might feel that I have been speaking flippantly. I can only reply that I have not offered the above examples in a frivolous spirit, nor do I feel them to be irrelevant. I do not wish to press them too far, for America and Israel are indeed far apart in time and space. But the only possible test of Noth's theories *re* aetiology must be made precisely where the facts are in our control. I should like to add, too, that the differences may not be as great as they seem. On the one hand, writing was known throughout the entire period of Israel's origins; on the other hand, in Colonial America schools and books were few, and illiteracy high. Oral tradition operated in both cases and, unless it be assumed that it operated in a special way in the ancient Orient, according to similar principles. Yet here, where we can keep check on the aetiological factor, it emphatically does not operate as Noth would have it. Therefore when I am told, for example, that the story of the circumcision of Israel at Gilgal (Josh. 5.2–9) is an aetiological legend to explain the later practice of the rite of circumcision at that shrine,[1] I am much less than convinced. Far more likely that the custom became popular at Gilgal precisely because of the tradition that great Joshua had once circumcised all Israel there. To say this, of course, neither asserts nor denies the historicity of that tradition; external evidence is required.

May I be pardoned another illustration? It offers, (*a*) a remarkable landmark, (*b*) a battle, and (*c*) a hero, as these have been enshrined in oral tradition. It was suggested to me by the arguments of Noth, Elliger and others[2] that the tale of the hanging of the five kings at Makkedah (Josh. 10.16–27) is an aetiological legend which grew up to explain a cave with its mouth blocked by stones and with five notable trees nearby.

I spent my childhood on the top of Lookout Mt, a steep and lofty eminence which towers above Chattanooga, Tenn. There there was fought in the course of 'The recent unpleasantness between the States' (as the Civil War used sometimes to be called), the

---

[1] e.g. Noth, *Das Buch Josua* (Handbuch zum AT; Tübingen, J. C. B. Mohr, 1938), 5f.
[2] See references in Ch. III n.[1] p. 64.

famous 'Battle above the Clouds'. Our home was scarcely a mile from the battlefield, and I wandered there often. The battleground itself consists of a narrow triangle at the 'point' of the mountain. Since the mountain's crest is rimmed everywhere with sheer cliffs some 50 or 60 feet in height, the land on two sides of this triangle falls precipitately away to the valley below; only on the side that opens along the ridge of the mountain is it more or less level. Now one of these cliffs in the mountain rim, the tallest and most precipitous of all, was known as 'Roper's Rock'. And thereby hangs a story.

Let me tell that story as I had it from oral tradition. For not until many years later did I even know that there was a written tradition. Confederate troops under Braxton Bragg—so the legend in oral form—had seized the height of Lookout Mt, and from it were pouring a murderous cannon fire into the city of Chattanooga below, much to the distress of U.S. Grant's Union forces who occupied it. Clearly Grant could not tolerate an enemy on this commanding height above him. So the decision was made to attack. Selecting a morning when a hanging mist rendered the valley invisible to the Confederates on the summit, Joe Hooker's Corps of Grant's Army deployed and began the assault. Halfway up, their presence was detected as they skirmished with Confederate pickets on the slope. Then the cannonade began. Shot and shell were poured into the assaulting Boys in Blue, but bravely they came on, scrambling up the sixty-degree pitch of the slope under fire. Finally they reached the ring of cliffs at the top and could go no farther. All seemed lost; the Blue line wavered. But just then there leaped to the fore the brave Sgt Roper, colour bearer of the NNth Pennsylvania (?) (or Ohio, or Illinois: oral tradition has forgotten the identity of his unit). Seizing the colours, he scrambled up a crevasse in the sheer rock, shouting the appropriate encouragements to his men as he did so. Bullets whined around him but, miraculously, none took effect. Finally to the top! Planting the colours in a crack, the sergeant grappled in mortal combat with the defending Boys in Grey (or butternut and old rags), while his comrades, thus heartened, swarmed up the cliff behind him.

At this point the oral tradition splits into two recensions. According to one, the brave sergeant, in the shock of the initial combat, was hurled backward from the cliff and killed. According to the other, he survived the battle unscathed and was decorated for his valour. In any event, Union arms forced the summit. The Boys in Grey did not retreat (that they never did!), but they did advance rapidly to the rear along the spine of the mountain, re- sisting stubbornly. So the principle of Union and the honour of the Lost Cause were both vindicated. And the name of the gallant Sgt Roper was given to the rock where he did his deed of derring- do, 'and there it is until this day!' So the oral tradition that I knew when I was a little boy.

But how could such a story possibly be true? The aetiology obtrudes like Roper's Rock itself, and this should be enough, if what we are told is correct, to render the whole thing suspect. Sgt Roper's deed is pure fancy, the Battle above the Clouds itself of dubious historicity. True, it is easy enough to see how such a legend could have developed. There is Roper's Rock, and it is a striking cliff; and people asked the natives why it was so called. And the natives, loath to be caught short by Yankee tourists, came up with the tale. Nor was it sheer, wilful fabrication. Tradi- tions of the Civil War hover like ghosts on the ridges about Chat- tanooga. It was natural for people honestly to suppose that the height of Lookout Mt, most commanding of all, had a part in the events. But the whole tale is fantastic. No competent general— and U.S. Grant, as even a Confederate might admit, was a com- petent general—would ever have ordered a frontal assault on so strong a position and, had he done so, it would never have suc- ceeded. Such a battle, therefore, never took place. As for Roper's Rock, we may suppose that its name derived from some pioneer family which once had settled nearby, but which had since re- moved and dropped from memory.

But what are the facts? First, that oral tradition has indeed vastly magnified the Battle above the Clouds. It was actually a skirmish, no more. The Confederates had scarcely more than 2,000 men, plus a few batteries of 12-pounders, on the summit. At most they could lob shells over in the direction of the railway station and scare the horses; they did the troops in the city no harm. But because their guns commanded the Tennessee River and could interdict Federal supplies moving on it, they had to be cleared off. But there was no frontal assault, no wild charge up the slope. Instead, Federal troops, covered by rain and fog, exe- cuted a sweeping movement that cleared Confederate outposts from the slope, leaving the troops on the summit invested on three sides. Nor was there any violent cannonade. The Confederate guns could not be depressed enough to be brought into play for, when this was done, the roundshot would roll out of the muzzles. Nor was there an assault on the cliffs. The Confederates, nearly cut off and virtually out of supplies, withdrew in the night. The next morning a Federal patrol reached the summit to find it vacant. Oral tradition has indeed exaggerated the events.

As for Sgt Roper, the tale of his gallant rush up the cliff cannot be historical: there was no assault on the cliff. Whether there was such a person as Sgt Roper, and whether he was the first of the patrol to reach the summit and plant the Union Flag there on the morrow of the battle, I do not know. Even if so, he performed no feat of heroism—except in so far as to climb such a crag requires a bit of nerve. Thus we see that we are entitled to look with a critical eye at the details of an oral tradition, particularly at any aetiological feature that it may present. But the mere presence of such a feature does not *per se* impeach the essential historicity of the events described. The aetiology of Roper's Rock is a secondary embellishment; the Battle above the Clouds, grievously exaggerated as it has been, certainly took place.

Noth, I am sure, would say that this is irrelevant. I do not think so. It is an example of the way in which folk tradition develops in oral transmission—for, I give assurance, I have known of Sgt Roper through no other source. True, this tradition comes from an age fully lighted by history. But that gives it an added advantage. It lets us see how oral tradition operates close to the source, within less than a century of the events, *and in spite of the fact that there has been a written tradition to control it since the very day of the battle*. Not even this last has prevented aetiological features from intruding. But these are seen clearly to be secondary. And the very fact that, where one can pin it down, the aetiological feature is, at least often, purely secondary, lays the burden of proof on him who asserts its invariable primacy in the traditions of Israel. This burden of proof, so far as I know, Noth has never accepted. He has asserted it to be so without a single scrap of evidence that it ever was so, and in the face of the fact that, where it can be tested, it can often be shown not to be so. For my part, I remain more than dubious that 'aetiological tales' ever at any time developed as the Alt-Noth school posits.

3. But to the third guiding principle of the Alt-Noth school: the stress on the *Ortsgebundenheit* (fixation in place) of tradition. Here again Albright has marshalled a quantity of evidence to the

contrary from modern Arab sources. I can add nothing to it. May I be permitted, however, to inject one or two other thoughts which he does not discuss?

The importance of *Ortsgebundenheit* in the method of Alt and Noth can hardly be exaggerated. All traditions have their *Haftpunkt*, some geographical locale to which they adhere, some cult centre at which they are handed down. This *Haftpunkt* can usually be inferred from places mentioned in the tradition, in so far as these cannot be shown to be secondary. This last can be a tricky business, to be sure. Thus the Jacob traditions are originally to be localized at Shechem (*UG*, 60, 86–95), and secondarily at Bethel, although it must be observed that this is achieved by separating the 'Transjordanian Jacob' from the patriarch and by regarding the links that connect Jacob to the Negeb as secondary (*UG*, 109 n. 289). Abraham and Isaac are localized in the Negeb (*UG*, 116f) —though, again, this is managed by ruling that the links that bind Abraham to Hebron, to central Palestine and to Mesopotamia, are secondary. Lot is localized in a cave near Zoar (*UG*, 168), Moses at a grave near Baal Peor (*UG*, 186ff). The conquest traditions of Josh. 1–9 are specifically Benjamite (all the events happen in the area of that tribe) and had their *Haftpunkt* at the great shrine of Gilgal.[1] That is to say, they are the property of the tribe to whose soil they relate—an hypothesis that rules out the possibility that any of them could refer to united action by more than one of the clans.

For my part, the very word *Ortsgebunden* has an almost mystical connotation that I quite fail to understand. True, place names in tradition are extremely tenacious. True, there *are* local traditions, in the sense that some traditions are developed locally, concern only local affairs, and do not tend to be of interest to a wider circle. But the very notion of a tradition being attached to a *place* is to me an incongruous one—a sort of mixed metaphor, if you will— while the doctrinaire consistency with which Alt and Noth apply the principle seems to me one-sided and unrealistic in the extreme. A number of objections can be raised.

First, aside from the fact noted above that the *Haftpunkt* of a tradition is often arrived at by eliminating evidence, it must be insisted that to establish the geographical locale of a tradition does not establish its *Haftpunkt*, but only its 'theatre of operation'. *All events happen somewhere*; and the fact that an event happened in a

[1] Cf. especially Alt, *Josua* (op. cit. in n.[2] p. 91), 183.

given area does not make the tradition of it the property of the people of that area nor fix the site of its transmission there. Is the surrender of the British at Yorktown a Virginia tradition because it has a Virginia locale? Or is the Declaration of Independence a Pennsylvania tradition because it took place in Philadelphia? The great theatre of the Civil War was Virginia. But is the Civil War a Virginia tradition? Of course traditions tend to be more cherished in the locale to which they refer (the Civil War is hard to forget in Richmond), *but they do not belong to, or inhere in, the locale; they belong to the people who participated in their making.* So, the mere fact that the bulk of the conquest narrative refers to Benjamite soil does not in itself say one thing about to whom the tradition belongs. It must be proved by other means that Benjamin, and Benjamin alone, was concerned in these events, before it can be asserted that the tradition is a Benjamite tribal one. But Alt and Noth merely assert it; they do not prove it.

Second, it is a demonstrable fact that traditions can shift location. Albright has given several examples from present-day Palestine, as well as one from the Bible: a tradition of Rachel's tomb both in the area of Benjamin and at Bethlehem (cf. Gen. 35.16–20; Jer. 31.15), no doubt because of confusion over the place name Ephrath. Alt and Noth themselves allow for this sort of thing: e.g. the removal of certain Jacob traditions from Shechem to Bethel (*UG*, 86ff). On the other hand, it is possible for a tradition to be perpetuated far from its original geographical locale, by a people who have no living contact with that locale.[1] It seems to me that here again we are dealing with principles which, if true at all, should be true of oral tradition anywhere, and which, therefore, may be discussed in the light of history on the basis of traditions whose development we can control. I therefore suggest the following examples.

We have already mentioned the legend of Washington's throwing the dollar over the Rappahannock. This tradition has long ago, like that of Rachel's grave, shifted locations. One often hears it said that Washington threw the dollar over the *Potomac*, and recently I saw this in print.[2] The reason for the shift is obvious.

---

[1] For example, some of the poems of Ras Shamra, notably the Keret Legend, though perpetuated in Ugarit far to the north, seem to have had their original setting in southern Phoenicia and the adjoining areas. Cf. the cautious remarks of R. de Langhe, *Les textes de Ras Shamra-Ugarit et leurs rapports avec le milieu biblique de l' Ancien Testament* (Paris, Desclée de Brouwer, 2 Vols. 1945), Vol. II, 97–174, 245f.

[2] In the syndicated newspaper magazine, *This Week* (Sunday, Dec. 13, 1953).

Washington is popularly more associated with Mt Vernon, on the Potomac near Washington, D.C., than with Fredericksburg on the Rappahannock. The tradition has followed the man. The fact that the Potomac at Mt Vernon is a tidal estuary more than a mile wide, and that no man living or dead could throw a dollar or anything else over it, does not trouble oral tradition. The tradition is not *Ortsgebunden*: not only did it transfer its location, *it is not handed down at either place*, but by the American people in general. Tradition moves with the people it concerns, and is transmitted by the people who feel participation in it.

Again: many of the folk ballads of the southern Appalachians have demonstrably been handed down in oral transmission from early settlers, whose forebears brought them ultimately from Elizabethan England, and that with a remarkable tenacity of content. But frequently the tendency may be noted to substitute local place names for the original English ones, with the result that English lords and ladies wander and plight their troth somewhere by the Forks of Big Sandy. Traditions can move, touch down anywhere and begin to assimilate the locale of the new environment. This again points up the fact that traditions belong not to places, but to the people who feel participation in them.

All this leads to the conclusion that, while place names do indeed have amazing tenacity, *Ortsgebundenheit* is a misnomer that ought to be given up. Traditions are not, and never have been, in any strict sense *Ortsgebunden* (tied to places); they are *Volksgebunden* (tied to people), if we may coin the term. They move through as wide an area as the people that transmit them move; their *Haftpunkt* is not a geographical location (admitting that traditions tend to be more cherished at the place where they originated), but the entire circle of people who feel personal concern in them.

It seems to me that, especially in the case of the patriarchal traditions, this stress on *Ortsgebundenheit* is dangerously wrong. Traditions adhere to people, and the people in this case were seminomads who, in the very search of seasonal pasture that Alt and Noth posit, must have roamed from one end of the land to the other. Therefore to localize the Jacob traditions in Shechem, the Abraham and Isaac traditions in the Negeb, and so forth, *is to localize people who, by their very manner of life, were not localized at all*. For my part, I see no *a priori* reason why traditions of Abraham, for example, that link him to Mesopotamia, Shechem, Bethel,

Hebron, the Negeb, Egypt, might not all of them be primary (though to say this does not, of course, in itself pass verdict on their historicity).

The mobility of the nomad must not be underestimated. True, the patriarchs were ass-nomads, not camel-nomads, and their wanderings were thus somewhat restricted. But even semi-nomads can get about amazingly. One might well think of the North American Indian in this connexion. These were for the most part semi-nomads, and that without benefit of beast at all (the horse was introduced relatively late, and then only on the Western Plains); they were canoe-nomads or foot-nomads. Yet if one reflects on their wide rangings, one will not be tempted to tie the ancient semi-nomad down too tightly. For example, Indians from Lake Superior and beyond traded furs regularly with the French in Montreal; in the 'French and Indian War', Indians from as far as the Mississippi and beyond fought in New York State under Montcalm. The range of the Hebrew nomads in the Pentateuch narrative: from Mesopotamia to Palestine, to the Negeb and to Egypt, is vastly more restricted. And we may assume that their traditions moved with them. In the light of all this, a doctrinaire localizing of early Israel's traditions at fixed *Haftpunkt* is most unrealistic.

4. Might one now venture, with all diffidence, a final and far more sweeping criticism of the method of Noth? Let it be put in the form of a question, namely: *even if this method be used with caution, is it in any event possible on the basis of present knowledge to write a 'History of Tradition' on the scale, and with the exactitude, that Noth attempts? And, if not, has a firm basis been found thereby for reconstructing the early history of Israel?*

Noth begins his study of tradition-history with the isolating of five major themes in the Pentateuch. Each of these he holds to have had separate origin and development from the others. *This is the pillar of the whole thesis.* Should it fall, the entire structure would have to be altered radically, if not demolished. But I should like to question precisely if the themes can so be isolated with the finality that Noth posits.

I do not wish to be dogmatic. The great unifying structure of Pentateuch history and theology was certainly imposed on the traditions relatively late (in *G*, but definitively in *J*); before that time, we may believe that individual traditions and blocks of traditions had their separate existence. Indeed, if one cares to press it, each individual tradition had its own separate origin and its own history of transmission before it entered larger cycles of tradition and, ultimately, the Pentateuch documents. One should not rashly deny the possibility that blocks of tradition—such as the Sinai traditions—may actually have had separate existence until a relatively late time. Furthermore, the five themes that Noth isolates are *there*, and one may certainly set them apart for the sake of convenience, if one wishes, much as one might isolate the major themes of a novel or a play, the better to grasp the whole. But do these themes have the real separation that Noth posits? For my part, I am not convinced.

Now four of these themes are already present in the ancient Cultic Credo of Deut. 26.5–9, and in Josh. 24.[1] That means that these themes were associated with one another back to a time, we may guess, soon after the conquest. That is to say, as far back as we have evidence they are *already together*. Notably absent, however, as both von Rad and Noth have pointed out, is the theme 'Revelation on Sinai': the Credo does not mention it. From this it is argued that this block of tradition was linked to the others only later. Noth, as we have seen, further deduces that exodus and Sinai events happened to different groups at different times.

The possibility that all this was so cannot be ruled out of court. But at least three observations might be made. First: failure to mention a tradition does not prove ignorance of it. For example, does the fact that so many of the Royal Psalms mention David, and David alone, argue that the Psalmist knew nothing of the other traditions of his people? Or does the fact that the primitive *kerygma* of the New Testament includes no reference to the Last Supper prove that the earliest church knew nothing of that event? Or does the fact that on Thanksgiving Day we mention the devotion of the Pilgrim Fathers prove that we never heard of Sir John Smith and the Jamestown colony? Second: it is likely that the Credo had its *Sitz im Leben* precisely in a regular ceremony of covenant renewal (cf. *GI*, 111). Note how the narrative of Josh. 24 leads straight to covenant: the mighty acts of God are recited that the people might then respond in reaffirming the covenant. Now it is in this ceremony, according to Noth himself, that the Sinai tradition was at home. There would be, then, no place in the Credo

---

[1] The theme 'Wandering in the Wilderness' is not explicit in the former, but it is in the latter (Josh. 24.7b). In any case, this theme has, I think, least right of all to separate existence.

for a recitation of the Sinai events; on the contrary, the people were expected to recreate those events, and participate in them, by their own act of covenant renewal. Finally: in the Decalogue itself (Ex. 20.2, Deut. 5.6) exodus and Sinai law *are* brought together.[1] Noth, of course, like many others, would deny that the Decalogue goes back to Mosaic days (*GI*, 111), but I must strongly side with those who take the contrary view.[2] But if the Decalogue represents the basic covenant law, then exodus and Sinai tradition are mated from the beginning. For these reasons one may doubt that the Sinai tradition was ever the separate entity it has been made out to be.[3]

No part of Noth's treatment is more prejudiced by the thesis of five separate themes than is his analysis of the Moses tradition. The figure of Moses runs through four of these themes, but it cannot be allowed that he was original in all, and thus the '*grosse Klammer*' that binds all together, else, as Noth tacitly agrees (*UG*, 177), the whole thesis would fall to the ground: a real independence of the themes could not be maintained. So the job is to find in which of them Moses is original. Nothing in Noth's work is more subjective than his procedure here. May I facetiously, but with dead seriousness, apply Noth's method to the figure of George Washington? I have no desire to try to reduce serious work to an absurdity, still less to make Moses and Washington identical figures. But it seems to me that any such hypothesis— and this is no more than an hypothesis—ought to be amenable to testing in the case of other historical figures who have been magnified in tradition, and who have extended themselves into many traditionary themes.

We may, then, isolate in the traditions of the Thirteen-Colony League six themes. (1) 'Settlement of the Wilderness': this theme has its nucleus in Massachusetts in the area of the Plymouth colony but, like the theme 'Patriarchs', has been expanded with similar material from elsewhere. Indeed, each of the thirteen colonies had its local tradition of migration, but most of these have been suppressed by the normative tradition. (2) 'The Brewing Storm': this has to do with the troubles leading up to the Revo-

---

[1] See the able study of G. E. Mendenhall, 'Covenant Forms in Israelite Tradition', *BA*, XVII–3 (1954), 50–76; cf. n.¹ on p. 82.

[2] Cf. H. H. Rowley, 'Moses and the Decalogue', *BJRL* 34 (1951), 81–118 for a defence of this view and full bibliography.

[3] A. Weiser, *Einleitung in das Alte Testament* (Göttingen, Vandenhoeck & Ruprecht, 2nd ed. 1949), 66ff, has also argued against separating Sinai and exodus traditions.

lution. It has its original *Haftpunkt* in the shrine of Boston, where the 'Tea Party' is celebrated, but it too has been expanded with traditions from elsewhere, notably from Virginia. (3) 'The Shot Heard Round the World': this tells of the outbreak of the struggle and has to do with such things as Paul Revere's ride and the fight at Concord Bridge. Its *Haftpunkt* is again the great shrine of Boston. (4) 'A Nation is Born': this centres about the formation of the Continental Congress, and the Declaration of Independence of 1776. It is a Pennsylvania tradition, its locale the shrine of Philadelphia. (5) 'Through the Night of Defeat': this is a Middle-American tradition and has to do with the dark days of 1776–8; its nucleus adheres to the pilgrim shrine of Valley Forge. (6) 'Final Victory': basically a Virginia tradition at home in the shrine of Yorktown, but supplemented with other material, particularly of Carolina origin.

Now Washington runs through all these themes save, of course, the first. But this cannot be original, else the thesis of separate themes falls. After all, it must be remembered that we are dealing with the traditions of the Thirteen-State League in normative form. It is quite natural, therefore, that Washington, being revered in all the states, has been drawn into all the traditionary themes. The task of the historian is to discover in which of them he is original. Let us proceed by elimination, as Noth has done.

Clearly Washington is not original in 'The Brewing Storm'. Indeed, he hardly appears here at all save as a militia officer under Braddock in the fighting around Pittsburgh. This, of course, is secondary: the effort of western Pennsylvania to have a part of the father of his country. The original figures in this theme are men like John Hancock and Sam Adams in Massachusetts, Patrick Henry in Virginia. 'The Shot Heard Round the World'? Hardly! Here again he is secondarily drawn in; indeed, his whole link to it is 'rather weak' (*verhältnismässig schwach*). He appears only at the very end to take command (July 1775) of the forces besieging Boston. But this is not historical; it represents the natural desire of the 'Hub of the Universe' to annex a bit of the national hero. Washington here has overlaid (as Moses at Sinai the elders of Israel) the humble and nameless heroes of Concord Bridge and Bunker Hill. 'A Nation is Born', then? Again, no! Indeed, Washington is weakest of all in this theme. He is introduced, to be sure; but one would expect that. The original figures were men like Thomas Jefferson and Ben Franklin. They were, alas, not military heroes, and so had to give place for the great leader. 'Through the Night of Defeat'? Washington is stronger here, but the explanation is simple. Since tradition had him to be the commander of the army in its final victory, it was naturally supposed that he was also the creator of that army. Of course, the original figure here is the crusty von Steuben. But he was a foreigner and the national hero overshadowed him. Then, too, because the fighting in the Middle Colonies was led for the most part by men who were grossly incompetent (Horatio Gates, Charles Lee), if not downright traitors (Benedict Arnold), these leaders tended to sink behind the immaculate and able figure of the hero.

But when we come to the last theme, 'Final Victory', it is clear that our search is nearing its end. For this is a Virginia tradition, and the figure of Washington is of Virginia origin. Even here, however, Washington is not original. The original heroes of Yorktown were lesser men: 'Mad Anthony' Wayne, perhaps, or Rochambeau, or de Grasse, or the debonair Lafayette. Washington has simply overlaid them. This, too, is easy to understand, for none of these men were Virginians; and local traditions tend to gather around a local hero. Actually, the *Haftpunkt* of the Washington tradition is a grave at Mt Vernon ('see, there it is until this day'). For, as Noth says (*UG*, 186), 'A grave tradition elsewhere usually gives the surest index of where a given figure of tradition is originally at home'. From this grave tradition the figure of Washington grew, as did that of Moses.

We may reconstruct the matter thus: Washington was an important squire in Northern Virginia and no doubt a leader of the struggle for independence there. But of his exploits we know next to nothing. He may have participated—though this is not certain —in some minor capacity in the fighting at Yorktown. But, since he was the ranking military leader of Virginia, Virginia tradition gradually exalted him above all the others, until he became the Commander of the Army and the architect of victory. Then, since Virginia early assumed a dominant position in the Thirteen-State League, the infant U.S.A., Virginia tradition naturally tended to become normative through the entire land. Thus Washington became the father of his Country and, as such, his figure found its way into all the traditionary themes.

But the reader has no doubt become impatient and has cried out, 'But this is preposterous! Furthermore, it is frivolous and is not to be taken seriously!' One can only reply: 'Precisely!' Certainly it is not to be taken seriously, nor should any sweeping conclusions be drawn from it. Washington is not Moses: he stands, and has always stood, in the full light of history. The traditions about him are not of the sort of the early traditions of Israel, nor was exodus and conquest a united action like the American Revolution. The point, however, is this: if what we have done with the figure of Washington is arbitrary, is what Noth has done with the figure of Moses any less arbitrary? Is the removal of Moses from the exodus theme, for example, anything but arbitrary? Could Noth's method of dealing with Moses be applied to any other figure of history without absurdity? And if to fragment the traditions of early America into separate themes represents a procedure patently absurd, what assurance is there that such an hypothesis has validity in the case of the traditions of early Israel? Noth assumes its validity as the basis of his whole tradition-history, but he can scarcely be said to have proved it. Yet if this assumption be not granted, the whole structure of his argument collapses. For my part, I find that structure so speculative that nothing can be based on it.

The trouble is that one cannot by direct argument prove Noth wrong. That is why arguments such as the above have been resorted to. But neither can Noth prove himself right. We move in a realm where we can no longer lay hold of objective evidence; we can only contradict one another. But the burden of proof is definitely on Noth. The entire structure of tradition-history rests upon certain assumptions, and deductions from those assumptions— no more. It is a very formidable structure indeed—until someone timidly pipes, 'But did it actually happen so?' In truth, there is no assurance that it did anything of the sort. There is no reason to assume that oral tradition followed such hard and fast rules, or that it developed at all in a manner so amenable to logic. Indeed, the amazing and incongruous thing about it all is that Noth is able, with but little objective evidence to go on, to give us the most elaborate and closely reasoned *Überlieferungsgeschichte*, telling us to the last detail how Israel's traditions developed—but he can give us no *Geschichte* of how Israel itself developed, for of this we have no information! It would seem that if the one can be reconstructed by hypothesis, so could the other. And if there is no data for writing the prehistory of Israel before the settlement—what shall we say of this *Überlieferungsgeschichte*?

It seems to me that objective evidence allows us to separate with some confidence the various Pentateuch documents. It allows us also, from a comparison of *J* and *E*, to posit a common *Grundlage* —though of its full content we cannot be sure. The evidence further requires us to assume that behind this there lay a long and complex history of oral transmission, leading from individual tradition, to larger cycles of tradition, to great traditionary sagas. In some cases, too, the evidence allows us to follow a particular tradition back to its original *Sitz im Leben*. But no more! It does not extend to a complete history of tradition. The attempt to write one represents, in my opinion, an extrapolation from the known data of a sort that sober method cannot consider permissible. I say all this, I repeat, with great diffidence, and with unabated admiration and respect for the scholarship of Alt and Noth, from whose work I have learned far more than I can begin to indicate here.

CHAPTER FIVE

CONCLUSIONS

WE have pointed out how the rise of the critical approach to the Old Testament posed a problem of method regarding the early traditions and the early history of Israel. We have reviewed certain current attempts to meet that problem and have concluded that they have not been wholly successful. The problem of the early traditions is not to be solved either by an abandonment of sound literary criticism or by an elaborate tradition-history: the former is on no account to be condoned, while the latter exceeds the evidence and plunges into subjectivism. What positive conclusions, then, if any, can be drawn? Since this is clearly not the place to attempt a detailed analysis of the traditions, still less a reconstruction of the events, we must confine ourselves to broad questions of method.

I

First of all, let it be submitted that the historian must be clear as to the nature and scope of his subject. Here we find ourselves continuing our discussion with Noth. For the question raises itself if he has not defined his subject wrongly, and therefore too strictly narrowed its scope.

Let us recall what Noth has said in the opening pages of his history (*GI*, 1–6). The name 'Israel' is properly the designation of the Twelve-Clan League. But since this Twelve-Clan League, as well as its component elements, did not take form until after the settlement, a history of Israel cannot begin until that point. Noth then goes on to ask whether Israel is to be spoken of as a 'people'. He lists three characteristics which, in his opinion, mark a 'people': common language, common habitat, and common historical experience. By the first two, Israel could be called a 'people' but, by the last, only to a limited degree. For, before the rise of the monarchy, the clans often acted independently and had vastly differing experiences; and, after the schism of the monarchy, Israel could not be said to have had a common historical experience again. Thus we may call Israel a 'people' only if we realize that we are employing the word in a special sense. Noth suggests that we dispense with the term altogether and speak simply of 'Israel'. 'Israel' means the Twelve-Clan League, and 'this twelve-tribe group constitutes, therefore, the subject of a "History of Israel"' (*GI*, 4).

1. This raises the question, first of all, if this is not to define the subject too narrowly. To be sure, one would agree that, aside from its use as the name of the eponymous ancestor of the people, 'Israel' appears for the first time as a designation of the Twelve-Clan League. Whatever prior application the name may have had, to some clan or group of clans, lies beyond our knowledge. We know Israel only as a Twelve-Clan League. But is that Twelve-Clan League really to be, as Noth maintains, 'the subject of a "History of Israel"'? If so, it would seem that the History of Israel would be a very short one. As Noth is well aware, the Twelve-Clan League was superseded by the monarchy and, with the consolidation of the state (which incorporated a host of peoples never members of any of the clans), became increasingly of vestigial importance. Indeed, as far as its practical functioning is concerned, it was abolished. True, it continued as a lively ideal of tremendous power, but the twelve-clan organization was not maintained, and clan affiliation became in most cases little more than a fiction. Now if this Twelve-Clan League be the subject of the history of Israel, Noth would be within his rights in beginning that history, as he does, with the normative constitution of that league. But, if he wishes to be consistent, he should end his history with the rise of the monarchy, and pursue thereafter the history of an idea.

Actually, of course, Noth does not follow any such procedure, and we should have been disappointed in him had he done so. 'Israel', as he points out, came to mean other things. It applied to the Davidic state, which was not coterminous with the Twelve-Clan League at all. It applied to the Northern State, but at the same time continued as a designation for all the people, north and south. Later it referred to the remnant of Israel, the Kingdom of Judah; later still, after the exile, it referred to the community of Judaism—as it still did in New Testament times and, indeed, does until today. So, while insisting that a history of Israel can begin only with the emergence of the Twelve-Clan League, Noth does not seek to end it with the desuetude of that league. But this raises the question if to equate 'Israel' with the Twelve-Clan League, and to deny it the definition of a 'people', was correct in the first place.

2. Is not Israel precisely a 'people'? This is not an idle question, but one that bears directly upon the scope of the historian's work.

Now a group may have historical existence, and so be the subject of a history, under any one of three headings: as a *race*, as a *nation*, or as a *people*. The first of these is essentially a biological designation, the second political, and the third primarily cultural.[1] The terms ought to be held sharply in focus if confusion is not to ensue. A *race* may be a minority or majority group within a given nation and/or culture (e.g. the American Negro, the Indians of Peru or Bolivia). It may, on the other hand, be distributed among many nations and cultures (e.g. the Negro race as such, the South American Indians as a whole). A *nation* may contain many races (e.g. the U.S.A., the U.S.S.R., the British Empire); it may contain many cultures (e.g. the British Empire, India, Bolivia, Peru). A cultural unit, however, may comprise many nations and races (e.g. Islamic culture), or it may be a minority within a nation or larger cultural group. (e.g. the Hopi Indians). And so on.

Under which of these headings is Israel to be classed? Surely not a *race*! Racially, Israel was a mixture from the beginning and in no essential distinct from her neighbours. One might as well speak of an Ohio race or a Virginia race! Was she a *nation*? Yes, but only for a relatively brief period. A history of Israel manifestly cannot be coterminous with Israel's existence as a state, or with any other form of organization under which she lived—and, by the same token, not with the Twelve-Clan League: the Twelve-Clan League *was a sort of political form*. In short, there seems to be no proper classification for Israel save as a *people*.

But if a 'people' is a cultural unit, what are the marks of 'peoplehood'? Are those adduced by Noth entirely correct? As for *common language*, one may agree that this is indeed one of the frequent marks of a cultural unit, and so may be allowed. But it ought not to be pressed too far. A cultural unit may, in the broad sense, cover many languages (e.g. Islamic culture, European culture). On the other hand, a cultural unit may be set off from its larger environment where no language barrier exists. Israel herself is a case in point. True, she had a common language through most of her history, but it differed only dialectally from that of her

---

[1] Cf. the illuminating discussion of the late R. T. O'Callaghan: *Aram Naharaim* (Rome, Pontifical Biblical Institute, 1948), 40 ff.

Canaanite neighbours, while there were dialects also within Israel. In any case, the distinctive mark of Israel was not her speech: it was not this that set her off from Moab, for example! Nor is *common habitat* an invariable mark of a 'people'. Granted that cultural groups more often than not occupy contiguous areas, granted that through most of her history Israel did so, is this really a necessary characteristic of a 'people'? One must say that it is not. One thinks of the ancient Greeks, who remained culturally a 'people' although scattered all over the world. Again are not the Jews of today similarly a 'people'? As for *common historical experience*, this is not a necessary mark of a 'people' at all, although it may frequently by coincidence be present. One thinks again of the ancient Greeks, who were certainly a cultural unit but who never at any time, save briefly under Alexander the Great (and then not the Greeks of Italy), knew any semblance of a common political experience!

This means that we shall have to get a better definition of a 'people'. But I should question if we will ever find an airtight one. To be a 'people' is to be bound together in a cultural unity; but the bonds that create such units are as various as the units themselves. They may be created by common language, common religion, common historical experience, common commercial interests—or any combination of all, or some, of these factors, and others besides. To discuss a 'people' requires that one in each case ask after those factors that draw it together into a cultural unit, and set it apart from all other units.

So, in the case of Israel, one must begin by asking: what is it that made Israel Israel? What made her different from her neighbours? For a unique phenomenon she undoubtedly was. And the answer is plain. It was not language, not habitat, not historical experience alone, not material culture—but *faith*. Israel was a people who became a people precisely because of her faith. The history of Israel, therefore, is not the history of a Twelve-Clan League, nor of a nation; *it is the history of a faith and its people*. It is, for that reason, a most serious omission when the attempt is made to write a purely political history of Israel, for this is to attempt a history with the fundamental factor of that history left in the background. That is another way of saying that the history of Israel and the history of Israel's religion are one and the same topic. The historian may, for good reason, lay stress on one side or the other, but never on one to the exclusion of the other.

2

This brings us to the question of the scope of such a history. If Israel be a people, specifically the people of a faith, then one must begin one's history with the beginnings of that people, and the beginnings of its religion. One cannot begin with the Twelve-Clan League in Palestine, unless one is able to demonstrate conclusively that neither people nor faith had existence prior to that time. That is, of course, precisely Noth's position. He holds that both the amphictyony and its component tribes took shape, and developed their normative Yahwism, after the settlement.

1. Now this position ought not flatly to be contradicted. We may not doubt that the Israelite amphictyony assumed its final and classical form only after the settlement. We cannot, I think, hope to argue that the conquest was a concerted invasion of all the clans as the normative tradition portrays it. Although the historicity of a violent assault in the thirteenth century is not to be denied, the evidence is too strong from the Bible itself that the conquest was also a long and involved process for this to be brushed aside. We might agree with Noth, too, that the composition of the various clans was fluid, and that those clans themselves reached stable form only in Palestine. I, for one, suspect that there was not a single clan whose later components were the children of people who had entered the land all at one time and in the same way. In this sense Israel did take shape after the settlement.

But had Israel and her clans no prior existence? It is impossible to debate the matter at length here. But one line of argument alone suffices to cast grave doubts on Noth's conclusions. I refer to the scheme of clan affiliation as it is given in the Bible (Gen. 29.14–30.24; 35.16–20). It is as follows:

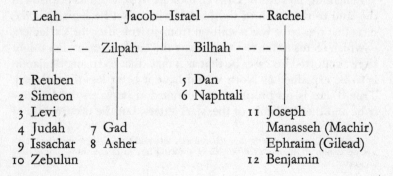

Leah ————	Jacob—Israel	———— Rachel
	- - - Zilpah ——⌐—— Bilhah - - - -	
1 Reuben		5 Dan
2 Simeon		6 Naphtali
3 Levi		11 Joseph
4 Judah	7 Gad	Manasseh (Machir)
9 Issachar	8 Asher	Ephraim (Gilead)
10 Zebulun		12 Benjamin

This scheme, to be sure, represents the final and normative clan affiliation. What its exact pre-history was we do not know. But it is most difficult to believe that such a picture could possibly have evolved after the settlement,[1] or that the clans themselves had no existence or common history prior to that time.

2. Noth argues (*GI*, 47f, 51, 57) that the tribes of Judah, Ephraim and Naphtali took their names from Mt Judah, Mt Ephraim and Mt Naphtali respectively, and so must have been formed in Palestine. One may agree that all the tribes took *final* form in Palestine. One may further agree that the etymology of these particular names is obscure. One may also agree that the Bible tradition posits that Ephraim arose late from a split in the Joseph tribe—and that this *might* have occurred after the settlement. But can it be proved that these tribes took their names from topographical features in Palestine? Such a procedure is not uninstanced (e.g. the Amorites). But the reverse is as likely to be true: a people can either take its name from, or give it to, a bit of geography. Examples of the latter process can be found all over the map of Asia and Europe, and could be listed by the page, e.g.: Canaanites-Canaan, Philistines-Palestine, Šardina-Sardinia; or Saxons-Saxony, Lombards-Lombardy, Angles-Anglia and England, Franks-Franconia and France, Germanii-Germany. Did the Mohawk Indians take their name from, or give it to, the river in New York State? Or was the Illinois River named after the Illini, or vice versa? And so on. Both processes are theoretically possible, and in the case of Judah, Ephraim and Naphtali either *could* have happened. But unless evidence can be produced that Mt Judah, Mt Ephraim and Mt Naphtali were so called *before* the arrival of these tribes, the matter cannot be settled, and no deductions should be based on it.

Benjamin, says Noth (*GI*, 53), took its name from its position in the land to the south of the Joseph tribes. But he denies (*GI*, 64, n. 2) that this tribe was a split-off from Joseph after the settlement —which seems to me to throw away the one argument that might have supported his case. Be that as it may, that the name Benjamin is to be explained as Noth would have it is far less than certain. True, there is no proof of any connexion between the Hebrew tribe and the Benjamin of the Mari letters, but the occurrences of

---

[1] Noth (*UG*, 109f) regards this scheme as a late and artificial construction. This lays upon him all the more the burden of showing how later conditions could have suggested it.

the name at Mari at least show that it is not predicated upon a fixed geographical position—certainly not in Palestine. The *banu-yamina* ('sons of the South') of Mari were not so called because they were to be found south of Mari.[1] About all the name Benjamin would prove is that its holder once circulated to the south of some one or some place, somewhere, at the time that it got the name. In other words, Benjamin could well have brought its name with it; it does not need to be explained by the location of that tribe in the land.

As for Issachar, Noth argues (*GI*, 56) that its name means 'hired man', and that this reflects the conditions in which that tribe found itself, as described in Gen. 49.14 f, after its settlement on the fringe of the Valley of Jezreel. Thus Issachar too was constituted in Palestine. But even were we to grant for the moment that this is correct, it would prove at most that the clan gained its name—a derogatory one—at that time; the possibility that it had had a prior existence under another name is not excluded. Indeed, Noth argues (*GI*, 67) that Issachar and Zebulun, since they are full Leah clans, must at an earlier period have been found farther to the south, in contact with Simeon and Levi (when these were in the Shechem area: Gen. 34), Reuben (likewise at one time west of the Jordan) and Judah. But this would mean that Issachar did exist *as a clan* before it supposedly got its present name, before its northerly migration. On the other hand, if there had not been some such prior contact with the other Leah clans, it is difficult to see why these two Galilean tribes would ever have been bracketed with them as full brothers. So we see that Noth's explanation of the name Issachar, even if correct, does not prove that that tribe arose only in Palestine. But is the explanation correct? It does not seem likely. Gen. 49.15 speaks of Issachar serving under corvée (*mas 'ôbēd*). Would a people subject to forced labour get the name 'hired man'? Are the two at all synonymous? Besides this, there is evidence for names developed from the same root as far back as the eighteenth century; it does not seem to mean 'hired man' at all.[2] There is, therefore, no evidence whatever that Issachar either

---

[1] Cf. recently C. J. Gadd, 'The Mari Letters', *Expository Times*, LXVI (1955), 174–177. The *banu-yamina* ranged far to the north of Mari. A tribe called the 'sons of the North' is also mentioned, but its location is not altogether clear.

[2] Cf. W. F. Albright, 'Northwest-Semitic Names in a List of Egyptian Slaves from the Eighteenth Century B.C.', *JAOS*, 74 (1955), 222–233 for the evidence and discussion (especially, 227 f).

received its name or took shape in Palestine; Gen. 49.15 is at most a word play.

Again, Reuben and Simeon are, in the normative clan system, the older brothers. This can only mean that in the formative period of Israel they were the most important clans. Now Simeon—together with Levi—was once, in an early phase of the occupation of Palestine, a powerful tribe indeed. Apparently it penetrated the Shechem area, only subsequently to be ejected and reduced to impotence. Noth argues that Reuben too was at one time west of the Jordan, but was pushed out. But, if this be so, it all occurred before the Joseph tribes occupied central Palestine, for Joseph settled precisely in the area that Simeon and Levi had once held. By the time the Twelve-Clan League was formed—and this could not have been until after the arrival of the Joseph tribes—Reuben and Simeon were, it would seem, of no importance. Simeon was driven into the Negeb and progressively absorbed in Judah; Reuben was forced east of the Dead Sea and, after the twelfth century (Judg. 5.15), virtually never heard of again.[1] Why, then, are these clans made the older brothers in the normative clan scheme when, in Noth's view, they were never of importance in or after the time in which the Twelve-Clan League was formed? Noth, who is aware of the problem, explains it by the assumption (*GI*, 77f) that Reuben, Simeon, and Levi were important members of a six clan 'Leah' amphictyony which flourished before the arrival of the Joseph clans in central Palestine. Although the existence of such a Six-Clan League is supported by hypothesis only, the hypothesis is not in itself implausible. In any event, an earlier phase of tribal history before the formation of the normative amphictyony is involved. There is not, however, a shred of evidence to support the assumption that these clans, and the affiliation between them arose only on the soil of Palestine. To suppose that they had had a common history while still in their semi-nomadic state is equally as reasonable.

As for Gad and Asher, the existence of the two, and a connexion between them, prior to their settlement simply has to be assumed. They are regarded as full brothers, sons of Zilpah, yet no two tribes had less physical connexion after they settled down. Where did this tradition of brotherhood arise? Not in Palestine—where one lay to the far east and the other to the far northwest! Why,

---

[1] Noth (*GI*, 54) argues that Reuben was still west of Jordan in the days of Deborah. The evidence is inconclusive, but it is not impossible.

furthermore, are these tribes reckoned as half-brothers of the Leah clans? Asher,[1] one might argue, settled adjacent to Zebulun —a Leah clan—and its link to Leah might be explained in that way. But why, then, a full brother to Gad? What connexion did Gad have with Leah clans in Palestine? True, she was adjacent to Reuben after the latter was pushed eastward, but this was in a late phase, presumably after contact with Asher had been lost. Further, Noth argues (*GI*, 64) that Gad entered the land as part of the Joseph movement; later she became mingled with Gileadites (*GI*, 52), part of an eastward back-migration of Ephraim. How, then, is Gad's Leah kinship, and her close relationship to Asher, to be explained unless one posits that these clans had a common history prior to their settlement?

Finally, Dan and Naphtali. The two are full brothers, sons of Bilhah and half-brothers of the Rachel clans. Since the two lived side by side after the Danite migration to the north, it might be argued that the tradition that they were brothers arose then. But, if so, how is kinship to the Rachel clans to be explained? To be sure, Dan was adjacent to Ephraim and Benjamin—Rachel clans— in her original area in the south. But Naphtali never had any direct contact at all with Rachel clans in Palestine. Now it is unlikely, in my opinion, that the Danite migration to the north was ever total; Danite families no doubt continued to maintain themselves in their original area as well. Thus, on the basis of conditions after the settlement, southern Danites might feel kinship to Rachel, but none to Naphtali; Naphtali might feel kinship to Dan, after that tribe's migration, but none to Rachel; only the northern Danites would feel kinship to both. It is far easier to believe that this sense of kinship reflects relationships between the clans in a phase before the settlement.

This has not, of course, exhausted the evidence. But it is enough, in my opinion, to cast grave doubts on Noth's views regarding the origin of the various clans and of the Israelite amphictyony. Not a single one of the clans can be proved to have arisen after the settlement; indeed, there is much evidence to the contrary. It would seem, further, that we must posit a common experience on the part of at least some of the clans prior to their arrival in Palestine.

---

[1] The name is not, as Noth suggests (*GI*, 55), a divine name, but of the root' *šr* ('blessed', 'happy'); cf. Albright, (op. cit. in n.[2] p. 17), 229 f.

3. If all this be so, it sets the scope of a history of Israel. We have reasoned that, since Israel is a 'people', specifically the people of a faith, her history must begin with the earliest beginnings of that people and that faith. The evidence, however, clearly argues that those beginnings lay back in the pre-settlement period. It must be assumed that the component clans of Israel existed in some form, with a common history on the part of at least some of them, before their arrival in Palestine. It must likewise be assumed, though the subject cannot be gone into here, that the distinctive faith of Israel had already been imparted to her in her desert days, and that the antecedents of it reach back to the religion of the patriarchs. Unanimous tradition, as well as archaeological evidence, points in this direction and reinforces our confidence that it is so.

It is, therefore, methodologically unsound to begin a history of Israel after the settlement in Palestine, with the emergence of the Twelve-Clan League in classical form. A history of the people Israel cannot be begun at that point any more than a history of the American people could be begun with the Declaration of Independence in 1776. True, before this last event there was, strictly speaking, no American people, but only a congeries of British subjects scattered through thirteen colonies. But the history of a 'people' cannot begin with the organization of that people under a normative form of government (and, let it be recalled, the amphictyony *was* a form of government, albeit *sui generis*); if it be the history of a 'people', it must go back to the beginnings of that people, and say what needs to be said of them, else it will fail in its purpose. A history of Israel, therefore, cannot begin with Israel in Palestine; it must go back, as do the biblical traditions, to the migrations of the patriarchs.

To be sure, the antecedents of Israel, unlike those of the American people, lie in the mists of antiquity. One is dealing here in a real sense, as Noth argues, with the pre-history of Israel, not her history. And that is always difficult. The story of the movements of semi-nomad clans is impossible to write to full satisfaction. For this reason we shall probably never be wholly pleased with our treatments of patriarchs, exodus and conquest. But we cannot give it up. *For the pre-history of a people is also a part of its history.* The historian may be dismayed at how little he can say with assurance, but that little he must essay to say. Noth, I am sure, would not disagree with this. The trouble is simply that his method has led him to such complete scepticism, both of tradition and of archaeological evidence, that he can say almost nothing.

3

But if the historian must attempt to treat the origins of Israel, what method is there to guide him? Here we are back to our initial problem. We can in these pages do no more than offer the reader a few statements of principle for his evaluation.

1. What is involved in describing the origins of a people depends, of course, on the people in question. In the case of an autochthonous people (if there be such a thing), the historian must seek by all the means at his disposal to penetrate into pre-history. He will examine archaeological evidence and attempt to trace the development of material culture. He will study material remains for what light they may throw upon possible contacts with other cultural areas, cultural breaks, population movements and the like. He will canvass later traditions for anything they may have to contribute. He will not overlook linguistic evidence for whatever it may have to tell concerning the affiliations of the speakers of such a language. And much more. So, for example, the historian of Egypt must proceed. For he cannot begin with the emergence of the dynasties and the earliest inscriptional witness; he must move backward through Chalcolithic and Stone Age cultures, and say what he can of origins.

In the case of a non-autochthonous people who have no tradition of origins, the problem is vastly more difficult. Such, for example, were the ancient Greeks, who came to their homeland in a series of migrations from the north, but who had apparently so completely forgotten this that they regarded themselves as indigenous. So, too, the classical Hittites who, so far as I know, had no tradition of their migration into Asia Minor, yet whose coming may in broad outline be established by archaeological evidence, and whose language—an Indo-European speech of the *centum* branch—betrays the general direction of their origin. Here the historian must canvass all available evidence of an archaeological, linguistic and cultural nature in order to say what he can about the date, direction and manner of their coming. He may be dismayed at how little there is to say, but he must say it; he cannot shirk it. Even if, as in the case of the Sumerians, his verdict must be a *non liquet*, there is no other course that he can pursue.

In the case of a non-autochthonous people who did have traditions of their origin elsewhere, the historian must proceed as above, but he must also lay those traditions down beside the other evidence and evaluate them in the light of it. He must ask if, so viewed, these traditions seem to be at all reasonable—seem to embody a genuine historical recollection. If such is the case, they become part of the evidence. True, they are not to be used uncritically; but neither are they to be ruled out of court.

Now the people Israel falls clearly into the last category. In fact, no people of antiquity had a tradition of origins even closely comparable to Israel's. This tradition affirmed that the ancestors had migrated from Mesopotamia, and were akin to the Aramean peoples there, with whom for a period they kept contact. It pictures them as pursuing a semi-nomadic, pastoral life in Palestine for some generations before wandering down to Egypt in time of famine. It then tells of hard bondage and the exodus miracle, of the march to Sinai, where was given the covenant and law that made Israel a people. Finally, it tells how they entered Palestine anew from the east and conquered it. The difficulties presented by these traditions must on no account be taken lightly. But the historian must begin in the period covered by them, must examine them in the light of all available evidence, and allow himself to be guided dispassionately by the balance of probability in the matter.

2. But how, specifically, are the Hexateuch traditions to be handled if the historian is to use them? A serious problem indeed! The traditions lie before us in a form received in the tenth century and after; they tell of events of the thirteenth century and long before. By what method is the gap to be bridged? First of all by analysis of the traditions. The historian will base himself on, and make full use of, the critical studies of past and present dealing with these traditions, in so far as these are sound.

That is to say, he will take his start from the approved methods and accepted results of literary criticism. How much of his labour in this area will be evident in his work will depend on its scope. But he will base himself on it. For it ought to be a first principle that the writing of history must begin with an analysis of the documents of history. To be sure, the once-fashionable over-nicety of analysis, and the drawing of elaborate deductions from it, is to be eschewed. Nor is the subject to be approached as if nothing had happened since Wellhausen. On the contrary, there must be full awareness of generations of labour, especially in the area of form criticism and in the history of tradition, which has modified a purely literary approach to the Old Testament. But the historian must not turn his back on what is sound in literary criticism. To do so is ruinous; it leads to uncritical results, if not to the abandonment of objective history writing altogether. In this respect, the historian must show himself the heir of the critical scholarship of the past.

But at the same time the historian will be aware that the documents are only the end result of a long history of transmission. In short, he will base himself also upon the insights of the post-Wellhausen development in the history of Old Testament studies. He will employ all objective methods, and gladly receive all objectively achieved results, which help to enlighten the pre-history of the traditions before they found final documentary form. This will include a comparison of *J* and *E* and the deduction of a possible *Grundlage* behind them, as Noth has done. It will especially include the numerous comparative studies of individual units of tradition, of a linguistic, topographical and archaeological nature, such as those in which the schools of Alt and Albright have been so prolific, which have done so much to illumine the original *Sitz im Leben* of those traditions. It will involve also an awareness of the literary form of the tradition, and of the rôle of oral tradition and the manner of its operation in selecting, refracting and stereotyping the tradition.

Beyond this, however, the historian will resolutely refuse to go. He will refuse to make unwarranted deductions which exceed the evidence, still less will he base the writing of history upon them. If this limits the amount that he can say, so be it! Specifically, he will realize that a complete history of tradition is impossible at the present—and probable future—state of knowledge. He will realize, too, that form criticism, in spite of its great value in the understanding and interpreting of tradition, can never of itself pass verdict on the historicity of tradition. It can help; but other factors must be brought into play.

3. How, then, is the historicity of the Hexateuch traditions to be evaluated? In the same manner, it would seem to me, as any other traditions are to be evaluated, namely by a balanced examination of internal and external evidence.

This is, indeed, the way in which one evaluates any story, any report, any bit of traditional lore, or whatnot. One examines its intrinsic probability and asks whether it at least sounds reasonable or not; one inquires what bias, if any, the teller of it may have had; one makes allowances for the form in which it is cast, for this might possibly have embellished the content more or less; one compares it with other forms of the same story, if any, that may have come to one's ears; and so on. But all this is extremely subjective unless external evidence can be called in. Is there any direct corroboration? Are there eye witnesses? Are there supporting documents? If none of these is forthcoming, one can only compare the tradition with what is otherwise known of the situation to which it refers and, with caution, strike the balance of probability.

Just so, fundamentally, are the Hexateuch traditions to be evaluated. The historian will ask after the intrinsic verisimilitude of the various traditions. He will not stop there, of course, for to do so would be a very subjective procedure, and one likely to reflect no more than his own predilections. But since the historian cannot quite get rid of himself as he works, it had better be mentioned. The watchword here is an open mind: one would do well neither to be gullible nor a professional sceptic. More objectively, the historian will make due allowance for the theological tendency of his documents, for the 'all Israel' framework in which the traditions are cast, and the like. He will take into consideration the form and type of each individual unit of tradition, and interpret it accordingly; and he will be aware of the epic nature of the whole. Moreover, making use of those traditionary units that comparative studies have shown to be very old (poems, lists, laws, etc), he may reconstruct to a certain degree the faith and constitution of Israel in the earliest period and use this for comparison with the picture presented in the various Hexateuch documents. And so on.

But the historian would be in a parlous position, and his evaluation of the tradition unconfirmed, if he could not appeal to external evidence. The external evidence here is that provided directly or indirectly by archaeology. To be sure, archaeological evidence regarding the pre-history of Israel is almost entirely circumstantial (i.e. without direct inscriptional witness to Israel). It does not prove any one of the traditions to be true in detail; to most of them it gives no direct witness at all. For that reason it is to be used circumspectly at all times. Yet far more positively than Noth would allow! If there is to be no glib 'proving the Bible true' from the side of archaeology, there is to be no disqualifying of archaeology in the interest of preconceived theory. The evidence from all sides is to be evaluated soberly and—again—the balance of probability is to be sought.

Now archaeology, it seems to me, bears on the early traditions from two sides: as regards certain individual traditions, and as regards the picture of the Hexateuch narrative as a whole. On the one hand, it casts light on certain particular points (e.g. the Nuzi texts and certain features in the patriarchal narrative; Palestinian excavation and the narrative of Josh. 5–10), and so is a witness to the general authenticity and antiquity of the tradition at these points. On the other hand, it has illumined the entire ancient Orient of the second millenium B.C., in the light of which the whole tradition of Israel's origins is to be read, and the nature of her early faith evaluated. To go into detail is forbidden here. Yet it must be repeated that, at all times, yet with due caution, external and internal evidence are to be held in balance; both are to be allowed their rightful voice in the evaluation of tradition. At the same time, pre-conceived theory regarding Israel's origins, of whatever sort and of whatever theological or philosophical bias, is to be resolutely eschewed.

The above are offered as no more than suggested methodological principles for evaluating the early traditions of Israel. Perhaps others could be added. There is, I feel, nothing novel or exciting about them. Indeed, they but carry forward the best in the history writing of the past.[1] Fundamentally, the only sound method is a careful examination of all the evidence, and the basing of conclusions upon it with all possible objectivity and a minimum of speculation. One may grant that this furnishes us with no rule of thumb for evaluating each tradition, still less with a master key to unlock the mysteries of the pre-history of Israel. In short, the early history of Israel remains at many points unknown; mere objectivity of method cannot provide all the answers. But if this is so, it is because objective evidence does not, at the present state of knowledge, extend to a complete solution. Nevertheless, objectivity of method alone can point us along the path that we must follow. It alone can give us solutions which, if partial, are at least soundly based.

To attempt to go on to a reconstruction of the origins of Israel, and to a detailed defence of the manner in which that is done, is beyond the scope of this study. Any reconstruction, as we have said, will leave something to be desired, so great are the gaps in

[1] I think especially of the work of Kittel (*GVI*) in this connexion.

our knowledge. Yet I venture the confidence that the broad outlines of the biblical tradition, and the essential content of the
Sinai faith, would be seen upon sober evaluation to be firmly
rooted in history. To attempt to recapture that history is difficult,
at times impossible, but it is no idle antiquarian employ: the very
foundations of biblical history and biblical theology are involved.

INDEX OF BIBLICAL REFERENCES

Bible Ref.	Page
Genesis	
1–11	42
3	93
11.27–32	49
12	62
15	48
15.18	62
16.13	48
19.30–38	50
22.1–19	91
23	48, 49, 92
24.62	48
25.7–10	92
25.11	48
25.21–26	93
25.27	47
26	48
28.13f	45
29.1	51
29.14–30, 24	115
31.42, 53	43
31.44–32.1	46
33.19	45, 91
34	40, 45, 51, 117
35.1–5	44, 91
35.16–20	38n 2, 45, 102, 115
48.22	45
49.5–7	40, 45
49.14f	117
49.15	38, 117, 118
49.24	43
50.10a, 11	46
Exodus	
2.1–10	93
20.2	106
23.31	62
24.1, 2, 9–11	52
Numbers	
13.21ff	62
21.21–35	62
32	62
32.36	49
34	62
34.1–12	62
Deuteronomy	
1–11	68
1.7	62
5.6	106
6.20–24	41
26.5–9	41, 44, 52, 105
27–34	68
34.6	53
Joshua	
1	63
1–9	39, 65, 71, 91, 101
1–11	57, 65, 66
1–12	39, 54
1.4	62
5–9	65
5–10	125
5.2–9	97
8.17	73
8.29	94
9.27	58, 68
10	57n 1
10.1–15	39, 39n 2
10.16–27	64, 97
10.26f	94
11	39
13.1–6	63
13.27	49
15.5–12	59
15.16	40

Bible Ref.	Page	Bible Ref.	Page
15.20–63	59	Judges	
15.45f	59, 60	1	57, 67
15.54	60	2–3	64, 69
15.60	60	2.1–5	63
16.1–3	59	2.20–3.4	63
16.8f	60	3	63, 75, 76
17.9f	60	5.15	118
17.14ff	39n 2	5.15b–16	40
18.17	40	20.1	63
18.21–28	59		
18.28	60	II Samuel	
19.40–46	59, 59n 2	18.17f	64
19.47	58, 76	I Kings	
20.7	38	3.2	58, 68, 69, 75, 76
21	60, 70, 74	II Kings	
22.19	62	23.15–20	60
23	67		
23.1–13	63	Psalms	
24	39n 2, 105	106.34	69
24.2–13	41	Jeremiah	
24.1–27	67	31.15	102
24.5	52		
24.7b	105n 1	Ezekiel	
24.28–33	67	47.15–20	62

INDEX OF BIBLICAL REFERENCES

Bible Ref.	Page	Bible Ref.	Page
Genesis		**Numbers**	
1–11	42	13.21ff	62
3	93	21.21–35	62
11.27–32	49	32	62
12	62	32.36	49
15	48	34	62
15.18	62	34.1–12	62
16.13	48		
19.30–38	50	**Deuteronomy**	
22.1–19	91	1–11	68
23	48, 49, 92	1.7	62
24.62	48	5.6	106
25.7–10	92	6.20–24	41
25.11	48	26.5–9	41, 44, 52, 105
25.21–26	93	27–34	68
25.27	47	34.6	53
26	48		
28.13f	45	**Joshua**	
29.1	51	1	63
29.14–30, 24	115	1–9	39, 65, 71, 91, 101
31.42, 53	43	1–11	57, 65, 66
31.44–32.1	46	1–12	39, 54
33.19	45, 91	1.4	62
34	40, 45, 51, 117	5–9	65
35.1–5	44, 91	5–10	125
35.16–20	38n 2, 45, 102, 115	5.2–9	97
48.22	45	8.17	73
49.5–7	40, 45	8.29	94
49.14f	117	9.27	58, 68
49.15	38, 117, 118	10	57n 1
49.24	43	10.1–15	39, 39n 2
50.10a, 11	46	10.16–27	64, 97
		10.26f	94
Exodus		11	39
2.1–10	93	13.1–6	63
20.2	106	13.27	49
23.31	62	15.5–12	59
24.1, 2, 9–11	52	15.16	40

Bible Ref.	Page	Bible Ref.	Page
15.20–63	59	Judges	
15.45f	59, 60	1	57, 67
15.54	60	2–3	64, 69
15.60	60	2.1–5	63
16.1–3	59	2.20–3.4	63
16.8f	60	3	63, 75, 76
17.9f	60	5.15	118
17.14ff	39n 2	5.15b–16	40
18.17	40	20.1	63
18.21–28	59		
18.28	60	II Samuel	
19.40–46	59, 59n 2	18.17f	64
19.47	58, 76		
20.7	38	I Kings	
21	60, 70, 74	3.2	58, 68, 69, 75, 76
22.19	62		
23	67	II Kings	
23.1–13	63	23.15–20	60
24	39n 2, 105	Psalms	
24.2–13	41	106.34	69
24.1–27	67		
24.5	52	Jeremiah	
24.7b	105n 1	31.15	102
24.28–33	67	Ezekiel	
		47.15–20	62

Thin
20 Nov. 1956.